THE DANCE Or DATA AND DELIVERY

CHOREOGRAPHING E-COMMERCE SUPPLY CHAINS THROUGH MACHINE LEARNING

SUBHARUN PAL

BlueRose ONE .com DIY
Stories Matter
NewDelhi • London

BLUEROSE PUBLISHERS

India | U.K.

For permissions requests or inquiries regarding this publication,
please contact:

BLUEROSE PUBLISHERS
www.BlueRoseONE.com
info@bluerosepublishers.com
+91 8882 898 898
+4407342408967

ISBN: 978-93-5819-961-1

First Edition: February 2024

Dedication:

To the unseen warriors of logistics and supply chain, who carry the weight of our world on their shoulders: each truck driver steering through the loneliness of endless highways, every warehouse soul counting treasures in the shadows, and the silent conductors of the colossal networks we seldom see. Yours is a labor of love and resilience, a silent symphony that keeps the heart of our world beating without pause. This book is a heartfelt homage to your tireless spirit, the unsung melody of our everyday existence.

To the dreamers and doers weaving the fabric of e-commerce with threads of code and data: the developers burning midnight oil over lines that hold worlds together, the data artists sculpting insights from chaos, and the seers envisioning a future more interconnected and fluid. May your code whisper secrets of success, your models evolve like living dreams, and your innovations fill the voids we never knew existed.

To the mentors and teachers, guardians of knowledge and curiosity: your words are not just lessons but lanterns in the dark, guiding a new generation to dance on the edges of the unknown, marrying data with soul and technology with the human heart.

To each person who has ever waited for a package with a hopeful heart: may this book unveil the hidden ballet that orchestrates your anticipation, transforming the impossible into everyday magic. May you discover in these pages a richer understanding of the grand dance of data and delivery.

And in the end, to the poetic union of technology and humanity: this book is a celebration of the enchanting dance of data and delivery, a testament to the miracle of human imagination and the precision of machines, forever a reminder of the wondrous symphony created when heart and technology move together in rhythm.

Subharun Pal

Acknowledgement:

At the heart of this journey, from a nascent idea to the pages before you, stands a constellation of extraordinary individuals whose support and wisdom have been the guiding stars for "The Dance of Data and Delivery." Their collective brilliance has turned a dream into a dialogue, a vision into a voice.

To my mentors and advisors, whose deep reservoirs of knowledge and sage advice have been the compass guiding this ship. Your profound understanding of both e-commerce and machine learning has been the lighthouse in the fog, illuminating the path from concept to creation. Your impact on this work is immeasurable.

To my academic peers, whose critical eyes and scholarly rigor have sharpened the edges of my thoughts and concepts. Your challenging questions and insightful critiques have been the anvil on which this work was forged. The professionals in e-commerce and supply chain sectors, your real-world perspectives have ensured that this book doesn't just float in the realm of theory but stands firmly on the ground of practical application.

A deep bow of gratitude to the editorial team and peer reviewers, whose meticulous and thoughtful feedback has polished this manuscript to its current luster. Your patience, encouragement, and unyielding dedication to excellence have been the wind beneath this book's wings.

To my family, my unwavering source of love and strength. To my spouse, Sharmistha, your emotional support and insightful critiques have been the bedrock of my resolve. To my son, Ayansh, your innocent curiosity and joyous laughter have been a constant reminder of the beauty in simplicity. To my parents, Malin Ch. Pal and Bina Pal, who sowed in me the seeds of diligence and perseverance, this book is a reflection of the values you nurtured in me.

A heartfelt salute to the unsung heroes of logistics - the delivery drivers, warehouse staff, and e-commerce professionals. Your daily endeavors make the intricate tapestry of supply chain logistics a living reality. This book is a tribute to your often overlooked, yet indispensable contributions to our daily lives.

And finally, to you, the reader, who embarks on this journey with me. Your engagement with this work gives it meaning and purpose. It is my earnest hope that "The Dance of Data and Delivery" offers you valuable insights and practical strategies to navigate and innovate within the dynamic realm of e-commerce supply chains through machine learning.

With profound and heartfelt thanks,

— Subharun Pal

Preface:

Welcome to the pages of "The Dance of Data and Delivery," a narrative that seeks to illuminate the hidden yet magnificent ballet of e-commerce. This book is not just a journey through the complex mazes of supply chains and the intricacies of machine learning algorithms; it's a voyage into the heart of a digital revolution that has redefined how we interact with the world.

In the era of instantaneous clicks and next-day deliveries, we seldom pause to ponder the marvel that makes it all tick. The digital age, with its convenience and speed, is underpinned by a symphony of processes, a dance of data and delivery that is both complex and beautiful. This book is an ode to that symphony, an exploration of the delicate pas de deux between human creativity and machine efficiency.

While many texts dissect the technical skeleton of e-commerce – the algorithms, data analytics, and logistics – "The Dance of Data and Delivery" aims to capture the soul of this digital behemoth. This is a narrative that transcends circuits and spreadsheets to delve into the artistry and strategy that breathes life into these digital entities. It's about understanding the poetry hidden within the binary, the human touch amidst the digital.

As you journey through these chapters, you'll encounter compelling case studies, insightful real-world applications, and engaging interviews with pioneers and visionaries. This isn't merely a collection of theories and concepts; it's a tapestry woven from rigorous research, rich experiences, and a deep understanding of the field.

Who is this book for? It's for the student with eyes set on the future of supply chain management and AI, offering a map to navigate the evolving landscape. For the seasoned professional, it provides fresh perspectives and strategies to stay agile in a rapidly changing market. And for the curious soul fascinated by the interplay of technology and commerce, this book is a window into the mesmerizing dance that shapes our world.

So, I invite you to turn these pages and immerse yourself in a world where data waltzes with delivery, where algorithms and orders perform an intricate ballet, and where you, the reader, become part of an exhilarating performance that is continuously unfolding.

Let the dance begin.

— Subharun Pal

Prologue:

In the quiet corners of a sprawling warehouse, hidden in the bustling heart of the city, unfolds a small yet profound miracle. Here, in this cavernous space, a computer algorithm—silent, vigilant, and intelligent—orchestrates a ballet of technology and human endeavor. It whispers commands to a robotic arm, which responds with a graceful swivel, deftly selecting a product from its shelf and placing it onto a conveyor belt. Thus begins the product's journey, seamlessly woven into the tapestry of countless others, all guided by an unseen symphony of code and data.

This is the world of e-commerce, a realm far beyond its humble beginnings. Gone are the days when online shopping was just a digital catalog, a convenient substitute for physical stores. Today, it stands as a dynamic, pulsating entity, an intricate fusion of technology, strategy, and human expertise that quietly underpins our daily lives. In this age, the ability to order a book, a pizza, or a piece of furniture from the comfort of home, and receive it almost as if by magic, is a testament to an invisible yet powerful dance.

But what is the secret behind the "Add to Cart" button? What mystical blend of data and decision-making powers this extraordinary spectacle of modern efficiency?

"The Dance of Data and Delivery" is a journey to unravel these mysteries. In its pages, we draw back the veil on the intricate choreography that sustains the digital marketplace of our era. This exploration is not confined to technology alone; it delves into the human decisions, the strategies, the subtle nuances that breathe life into a predominantly data-driven operation. As you delve deeper, you will be privy to the elegant ballet of bytes and boxes, a meticulously choreographed performance harmonizing algorithms, supply chains, and the human touch.

This narrative invites you to witness how machine learning and human creativity twirl in perfect unison, transforming the cumbersome gears of e-commerce into a fluid whirlwind of efficiency, sustainability, and customer delight.

So, dear reader, embark on this enlightening journey. Welcome to the mesmerizing world of "The Dance of Data and Delivery," where every page turn reveals the artful harmony of machines and humanity, technology and commerce, complexity and simplicity.

Welcome to the dance of the future.

— Subharun Pal

Poetic Blurb:

IIn the vast digital expanse, where bytes and bits waltz in an unseen sky,

A mesmerizing dance unfolds, a spectacle where data and delivery intertwine.

Here, on the grand stage of e-commerce, entangled with complex supply chains,

Machine Learning stands as the maestro, orchestrating with precision, never in vain.

With every algorithm, a graceful symphony arises,

Choreographing a ballet of movements through the vastness of cyberspace.

This dance floor, a vibrant canvas of logistical dreams,

Is painted with the codes of innovation, fulfilling desires unseen.

In this enchanting dance of deliverance, intricate patterns gracefully emerge,

As predictive analytics waltz on the edge of discovery, crafting experiences that converge.

Personalized journeys unfold on the e-commerce stage, serene,

Creating a world where each step is tailored, each pathway unseen.

Whirling and twirling in a harmonious spree,

Data and delivery flow as rhythmically as the sea.

In this ballet of bytes, watch as wonders align,

With Machine Learning the maestro of this dance so divine.

Beneath the glow of the digital moon's soft light,

Silhouettes of supply chains move in tune through the night.

With each step, a melody of progress and boon resonates in the room,

"The Dance of Data and Delivery," a harmonious monsoon of bloom.

About the Author:

Subharun Pal, a luminary in the academic and technological spheres, melds scholarly depth with methodological precision in the dynamic field of e-commerce and machine learning. His academic odyssey is distinguished by affiliations with globally esteemed institutions, including the Swiss School of Management (SSM) in Switzerland and the European International University (EIU) in France. His expertise encompasses a vast array of disciplines, ranging from computer science engineering to disruptive technology, operations management, logistics, supply chain orchestration, fiscal analytics, commercial jurisprudence, and educational philosophy.

Pal's academic contributions are further enriched by his associations with premier educational establishments worldwide. His collaborations span across notable Indian institutions like IIT Jammu, IIT Patna, IIM Calcutta, IIM Ranchi, the National University of Juridical Sciences Kolkata, Karnataka State Open University Mysore, and Visvesvaraya Technological University Belgaum, as well as international universities such as Edith Cowan University in Perth. Additionally, his engagement with the CII-Institute of Logistics in Chennai highlights his commitment to specialized knowledge in logistics and supply chain management.

Renowned for his intellectual acuity, Pal's work has garnered recognition and endorsements from esteemed global entities such as The World Bank, KPMG, Cisco, Microsoft, and Oracle. His scholarly portfolio boasts an extensive array of research papers, insightful treatises, and groundbreaking patents, reflecting his profound influence both internationally and within India.

As an author, editor, and thought leader, Pal has played a pivotal role in academic symposia and has contributed significantly to editorial projects, reinforcing his dedication to advancing various academic disciplines. His relentless pursuit of knowledge and excellence has solidified his reputation within the international scholarly community and earned him numerous accolades, marking him as a distinguished figure in the global intellectual landscape.

In his seminal work, "The Dance of Data and Delivery: Choreographing E-Commerce Supply Chains Through Machine Learning," Pal brings together his comprehensive academic background and practical insights, offering readers a groundbreaking perspective on the intersection of technology and commerce.

Table of Contents

Chapter 1:
Unveiling the Synergy: E-Commerce Supply Chains & Machine Learning

Introduction

In the dynamic and ever-evolving world of e-commerce, the supply chain is not merely a logistic mechanism but rather the foundational framework supporting the entire business model. The advent of Machine Learning (ML) has heralded a new era in these supply chains, bringing about a paradigm shift characterized by enhanced efficiency, precision, and adaptability. This chapter offers an in-depth exploration of the symbiotic relationship between ML and e-commerce supply chains. It delves into how ML is revolutionizing traditional logistics paradigms, significantly improving various aspects such as inventory management, order processing, transportation logistics, and customer satisfaction.

The Evolution of E-Commerce Supply Chains

The rise of e-commerce has been meteoric, fueled by advances in technology and shifts in consumer behavior. This sector's growth necessitated a fundamental transformation in supply chains, which historically catered to physical storefronts. Contemporary e-commerce supply chains now embody a complex matrix of processes including sourcing, inventory management, warehousing, order processing, transportation, and customer service.

Each component of this supply chain has evolved to meet the specific demands of online retail, such as the need for faster delivery options, more dynamic inventory management systems, and seamless integration of customer service experiences. This evolution represents a significant departure from traditional supply chain models, reflecting a more agile, responsive, and customer-centric approach.

Integrating Machine Learning into E-Commerce Supply Chains

Machine Learning emerges as a transformative force within these supply chains. ML algorithms, driven by data analytics and pattern recognition, automate and optimize processes, contributing to real-time decision-making and operational efficiency.

- Inventory Management through Predictive Analytics: ML algorithms provide sophisticated predictive analytics, enabling businesses to forecast demand with greater accuracy. This capability is pivotal in managing inventory levels, mitigating risks of overstocking or stockouts, and aligning product availability with consumer demand trends.

- Warehousing Optimization: ML substantially enhances warehousing operations. It includes the automation of sorting and storage systems, optimization of space utilization, and efficient picking processes. These advancements lead to significant reductions in order processing times and operational costs.

- Dynamic Pricing and Demand Forecasting: Utilizing ML for dynamic pricing and demand forecasting involves analyzing extensive datasets covering market trends, consumer purchasing behaviors, and sales histories. This analysis informs strategic pricing decisions and accurate demand predictions, vital for maintaining competitive advantage and operational resilience.

- Transportation and Logistics Efficiency: ML optimizes logistics by enhancing route planning, predicting transit times, and managing logistic networks more effectively. These improvements contribute to cost reductions, timely deliveries, and increased customer satisfaction, which are critical in the e-commerce domain.

- Advancing Customer Service: The application of ML in customer service, through tools like intelligent chatbots and personalized recommendation systems, provides a more engaging and customized shopping experience. These innovations not only elevate customer satisfaction but also foster brand loyalty and repeat business.

Challenges and Future Perspectives

Despite its numerous advantages, integrating ML into e-commerce supply chains presents challenges. These include concerns around data privacy and security, the need for specialized personnel to manage and interpret complex ML systems, and the necessity to continually adapt to rapidly evolving technologies. The future trajectory of e-commerce supply chains will likely involve a deeper integration of ML with other emerging technologies, such as blockchain and the Internet of Things (IoT), to create even more robust, efficient, and customer-centric systems.

Conclusion

This chapter has illuminated the profound impact of machine learning on the domain of e-commerce supply chains. The synergy between ML and these supply chains is not just enhancing current processes but is also setting the stage for innovative operational strategies. As the e-commerce sector continues its upward trajectory, the role of ML in supply chain management will become increasingly pivotal, fundamentally shaping the future of online retail.

Chapter 2:
Choreographing Success: The Rhythm of Machine Learning Models & Techniques

Introduction

In the dynamic world of e-commerce, machine learning (ML) models and techniques are akin to a rhythm that orchestrates the dance of success. This chapter delves deeply into the various ML models and techniques that play a pivotal role in enhancing e-commerce operations. It explores their applications, the value they add to different aspects of e-commerce, and how they are transforming the landscape of online retail.

Understanding Machine Learning Models

- Supervised Learning: This approach is similar to teaching a child using examples. The model is trained on a dataset where each piece of data is tagged with the correct answer. In e-commerce, applications of supervised learning include sophisticated product recommendation systems and intricate customer sentiment analysis.

- Unsupervised Learning: In this model, the algorithm autonomously discovers patterns and relationships within the data. This technique is invaluable for segmenting customers into distinct groups based on their purchasing behaviors, providing a foundation for targeted and effective marketing strategies.

- Reinforcement Learning: Operating on a trial-and-error basis, this model fine-tunes its actions based on feedback to maximize rewards. It finds application in e-commerce for optimizing dynamic pricing models, where the algorithm progressively learns the most effective pricing strategy.

Key Machine Learning Techniques in E-Commerce

- Classification and Regression: Fundamental in predicting customer behaviors, classification algorithms categorize data, such as predicting customer churn, while regression algorithms are used to predict numerical values like sales forecasts.

- Clustering: This technique is central to customer segmentation, identifying clusters of customers with similar behaviors or preferences for targeted marketing strategies.

- Natural Language Processing (NLP): NLP is essential for parsing customer feedback and queries. It powers sophisticated chatbots and sentiment analysis tools, facilitating automated customer service and gaining insights into customer sentiments regarding products or services.

- Neural Networks and Deep Learning: These advanced techniques are adept at handling complex tasks such as image recognition for product categorization and creating personalization algorithms that suggest products based on a customer's browsing history and preferences.

- Anomaly Detection: Employed for detecting fraud in transactions, this technique identifies unusual patterns that could indicate fraudulent activities.

Implementing Machine Learning Techniques in E-Commerce

The implementation of these ML techniques in e-commerce involves a comprehensive process:

- Data Collection and Preparation: Gathering relevant data from various sources and preprocessing it into a format suitable for ML algorithms.

- Model Selection and Training: Choosing the most appropriate models for the specific e-commerce application and training them with the prepared dataset.

- Evaluation and Tuning: Rigorously assessing the model's performance and fine-tuning its parameters to enhance accuracy and efficiency.

- Deployment and Continuous Monitoring: Integrating the model into the e-commerce ecosystem, followed by continuous monitoring and adjustments to maintain optimal performance.

Challenges and Considerations

The adoption of ML in e-commerce presents several challenges. It requires substantial investment in technology infrastructure and skilled personnel. Data privacy and ethical considerations in the usage of customer data are critical. Moreover, these models need constant updates to stay aligned with evolving market trends and consumer behaviors.

Conclusion

Machine learning models and techniques are the vital pulse of modern e-commerce operations, driving innovation and efficiency across various facets. From refining customer experiences to streamlining logistics and beyond, their applications are extensive and transformative. As the e-commerce landscape continues to evolve, the sophistication and impact of these ML-driven solutions are poised to scale new heights, heralding an exciting future for online retail.

Chapter 3:
The Bedrock of Innovation: Exploring the Foundations of Machine Learning

Introduction

In the ever-evolving landscape of e-commerce supply chains, machine learning stands as a cornerstone of innovation. As we delve into "The Dance of Data and Delivery: Choreographing E-commerce Supply Chains through Machine Learning," it is essential to understand the foundations of machine learning, which drives this transformation. This article aims to explore the fundamental aspects of machine learning, its core concepts, and its revolutionary impact on e-commerce supply chains.

Understanding Machine Learning: The Basics

Definition and Evolution

- Machine Learning Defined: At its core, machine learning is a branch of artificial intelligence (AI) that gives computers the ability to learn and adapt through experience without being explicitly programmed. It focuses on the development of algorithms that can process input data and use statistical analysis to predict an output.

- Historical Evolution: The journey of machine learning is intertwined with the history of AI, starting from the early days of simple pattern recognition. Significant milestones include the development of neural networks in the 1950s, the advent of the perceptron in the 1960s, and the emergence of decision trees in the 1980s.

The resurgence of neural networks in the form of deep learning in the 21st century marked a pivotal point, leading to breakthroughs in various fields, including supply chain management.

Key Concepts and Algorithms

Algorithms at Play

- Decision Trees: These are tree-like models used for classification and regression. In supply chain management, decision trees can help in making decisions about stock levels, logistics, and even in customer service scenarios.

- Neural Networks: Inspired by the human brain, neural networks are a series of algorithms that recognize underlying relationships in a set of data. They are particularly useful in complex problem-solving scenarios in supply chains, such as predicting shipping delays or identifying inefficiencies in operations.

- Support Vector Machines (SVMs): SVMs are supervised learning models used for classification and regression analysis. In supply chains, SVMs can be employed for quality assurance, categorizing products based on quality metrics.

Data: The Fuel for Machine Learning

- Importance of Data Quality: The effectiveness of machine learning algorithms is heavily dependent on the quality of data they are trained on. Inaccurate or incomplete data can lead to poor decision-making in supply chains.

- Data Quantity and Diversity: Large volumes of diverse data can significantly improve the learning process, allowing algorithms to capture various aspects of supply chain operations. This includes data from internal operations, market trends, and customer feedback.

- Data Preprocessing: Preprocessing involves cleaning and transforming raw data into an understandable format. Proper preprocessing is crucial in supply chain contexts to ensure that the input data accurately reflects the operational realities.

Machine learning's role in enhancing e-commerce supply chains cannot be overstated. Its foundational elements – from core algorithms to the pivotal role of data – underpin the sophisticated analytics and automation driving modern supply chains. Understanding these basics is essential for leveraging machine learning's full potential in optimizing e-commerce operations.

Machine Learning in E-commerce Supply Chains

Demand Forecasting and Inventory Management

- Enhanced Demand Prediction: Machine learning algorithms excel at analyzing historical sales data, market trends, and consumer behaviors to forecast future product demand with high accuracy. This predictive capability allows for more efficient inventory management, reducing overstock and stockouts.

- Dynamic Inventory Replenishment: Machine learning enables dynamic inventory replenishment systems that can automatically adjust ordering patterns based on predicted demand, thereby optimizing inventory levels and minimizing waste.

Personalization and Customer Experience

- Customized Product Recommendations: Machine learning algorithms analyze customer data and purchasing history to provide tailored product recommendations, enhancing the shopping experience and increasing sales.

- Dynamic Pricing Models: Using machine learning for dynamic pricing allows e-commerce platforms to adjust prices in real-time based on demand, competition, customer behavior, and market conditions, maximizing profitability and customer engagement.

Logistics Optimization

- Route Optimization: Machine learning algorithms can optimize delivery routes by considering factors like traffic patterns, distance, delivery windows, and vehicle capacity, thus reducing delivery times and costs.

- Predictive Maintenance in Logistics: Predictive analytics in machine learning enables anticipatory maintenance of logistics infrastructure, such as vehicles and machinery, thus reducing downtime and prolonging equipment life.

Challenges and Considerations

Data Privacy and Security

- Safeguarding Consumer Data: Ensuring the privacy and security of consumer data used in machine learning applications is critical, requiring adherence to data protection regulations and the implementation of robust cybersecurity measures.

- Ethical Data Use: Addressing ethical concerns related to the use of consumer data in machine learning algorithms, such as avoiding biases and respecting consumer privacy rights.

Integration with Existing Systems

- Compatibility and Interoperability: Overcoming the challenge of integrating machine learning solutions with existing supply chain and IT infrastructure, which may require system upgrades or the use of middleware.

- Change Management: Managing the organizational change that comes with integrating new technologies, including training employees and modifying existing processes.

Future Perspectives and Advancements

Advancements in AI and ML Technologies

- Evolution of Deep Learning: Advancements in deep learning and neural networks are expected to further enhance the accuracy and efficiency of predictive models in supply chain management.

- Natural Language Processing (NLP): Continued improvements in NLP will enable more sophisticated customer service chatbots and improved sentiment analysis for better understanding of customer feedback.

Emerging Trends

- AI-driven Automation: The increasing trend towards AI-driven automation in supply chain processes, including automated warehousing and AI-based logistics management.

- Predictive Analytics for Customer Behavior: Advanced predictive analytics leveraging machine learning to understand and anticipate customer behaviors, enabling more effective marketing and product development strategies.

- IoT and Machine Learning Convergence: The growing integration of IoT with machine learning, leading to more connected, responsive, and intelligent supply chain operations.

The role of machine learning in revolutionizing e-commerce supply chains is undeniable. From refining inventory management and personalizing customer experiences to optimizing logistics, its impact is extensive. However, these advancements come with their challenges, notably in data privacy and systems integration. Looking forward, continuous innovations in AI and ML promise to further enhance the efficiency and responsiveness of e-commerce supply chains, aligning with emerging trends and consumer expectations.

Conclusion

Machine learning stands as the bedrock of innovation in the realm of e-commerce supply chains. Its ability to process vast amounts of data, learn patterns, and make informed decisions is transforming how supply chains operate. From enhancing customer experiences to optimizing logistics and inventory management, the impact of machine learning is profound and far-reaching. However, this journey is not without challenges, such as data privacy concerns and the need for seamless integration with existing systems. Looking ahead, the continual advancements in machine learning promise even more remarkable transformations in e-commerce supply chains. Embracing these innovations, while navigating their challenges, will be key to leveraging the full potential of machine learning in this dynamic industry. "The Dance of Data and Delivery" is an ongoing performance, with machine learning as its lead choreographer, orchestrating a more efficient, responsive, and intelligent supply chain ecosystem.

Chapter 4:
Data Dynamics: The Pulse of Machine Learning

Introduction

In the digital symphony of e-commerce supply chains, machine learning (ML) plays a leading role, with data serving as its lifeblood. The book "The Dance of Data and Delivery: Choreographing E-commerce Supply Chains through Machine Learning" delves deep into this interplay. This article, "Data Dynamics: The Pulse of Machine Learning," explores the critical role of data in powering machine learning algorithms and how this synergy drives the optimization of e-commerce supply chains.

The Essence of Data in Machine Learning

Role and Importance

- Data as the Building Block: In the context of machine learning, data is akin to a building block that shapes the learning and effectiveness of algorithms. It's through data that these algorithms can identify patterns, make predictions, and support decision-making processes.

- Diverse Data Sources: In e-commerce supply chains, data sources are extensive and varied. This includes not only transactional records but also real-time logistics data, supplier performance metrics, customer browsing behaviors, and social media interactions. Each source contributes a unique piece to the overall picture.

Data Quality and Quantity

- Ensuring Data Integrity: The integrity of data, characterized by its accuracy, completeness, and consistency, is crucial. Poor data quality can lead to misleading ML outcomes, which in turn can affect supply chain decisions and customer satisfaction.

- Volume and Variety: The volume of data and its variety (structured and unstructured) also play a critical role. Large datasets help in building more robust ML models, while a variety of data enhances the model's ability to handle complex, multifaceted supply chain scenarios.

Data Collection and Processing

Sources of Data

- Omni-Channel Data Collection: Modern e-commerce operations are omni-channel, meaning data collection spans across online platforms, mobile apps, in-store interactions, and more. Each channel provides valuable insights for ML algorithms.

- Real-Time Data Streams: Real-time data streams from IoT devices in logistics and warehouses offer up-to-the-minute information for agile decision-making.

Data Processing Techniques

Advanced Processing Tools: Leveraging advanced data processing tools and technologies like data warehousing, ETL (Extract, Transform, Load) processes, and cloud-based analytics platforms.

Ensuring Data Relevance: The relevance of data is maintained through techniques like data pruning, where irrelevant or redundant data is removed, ensuring that ML models are trained on pertinent data.

Machine Learning Algorithms in Data Analysis

Predictive Analytics

Enhanced Demand Forecasting: Using ML for advanced demand forecasting, which considers not just historical sales but also external factors like market trends, economic indicators, and consumer preferences.

Inventory Optimization: Application of ML in predictive analytics for inventory optimization, anticipating stock requirements more accurately and reducing the risk of overstocking or understocking.

Pattern Recognition

- Fraud Detection: Using ML algorithms for fraud detection by identifying unusual patterns or deviations from the norm in transaction data.

- Customer Segmentation: Employing ML for sophisticated customer segmentation, enabling more targeted and effective marketing strategies.

Enhancing Supply Chain Operations with Data-Driven Insights

Operational Efficiency

- Automated Decision Making: Implementing ML-driven automated decision-making systems for operational tasks such as order fulfillment, procurement, and logistics management.

- Supply Chain Resilience: Enhancing supply chain resilience by using ML to identify potential disruptions and develop proactive strategies.

Customer-Centric Approaches

- Personalization at Scale: Utilizing ML to offer personalized experiences at scale, from customized product recommendations to tailored marketing messages.

- Customer Journey Analytics: Analyzing the end-to-end customer journey through ML to identify opportunities for improvement in service delivery.

Overcoming Data Challenges in Machine Learning

Data Privacy and Security

- Regulatory Adherence: Staying compliant with evolving data privacy regulations like GDPR and ensuring that data handling practices are transparent and secure.

- Advanced Security Protocols: Implementing advanced security protocols and encryption techniques to safeguard data against breaches and unauthorized access.

Dealing with Incomplete or Biased Data

- Data Augmentation: Employing data augmentation techniques to address issues of incomplete data, thereby enhancing the quality and effectiveness of ML models.

- Bias Detection and Mitigation: Actively working to detect and mitigate biases in data, ensuring that ML algorithms make fair and unbiased decisions.

By understanding and effectively managing the nuances of data dynamics, e-commerce businesses can leverage machine learning to revolutionize their supply chain operations, making them more efficient, responsive, and customer focused. The successful application of ML in this domain hinges on the quality, processing, and ethical use of data, underscoring its role as the pulse of machine learning innovation.

Conclusion

Data serves as the pulsating heart of machine learning algorithms, driving the advanced capabilities that are transforming e-commerce supply chains. The synergy of data dynamics and machine learning leads to more intelligent, efficient, and responsive supply chain operations, aligning closely with customer needs and market demands. While challenges like data privacy, security, and quality persist, overcoming them is key to harnessing the full potential of machine learning in e-commerce. As we advance, the role of data in shaping the future of supply chain management will only grow more pronounced, making its effective use a cornerstone of success in the ever-evolving landscape of e-commerce.

Chapter 5:
Future-Proofing Inventory: The Role of Predictive Analytics

Introduction

In the rapidly evolving e-commerce sector, inventory management is a critical yet challenging task, requiring a delicate balance between supply and demand. Predictive analytics, an advanced application of machine learning, is significantly altering this landscape. This chapter delves into the transformative role of predictive analytics in inventory management, illustrating how it empowers businesses to anticipate future demand, optimize inventory levels, and navigate the complexities of overstocking and stockouts.

The Essence of Predictive Analytics in Inventory Management

Predictive analytics is a sophisticated analytical approach that combines historical data, statistical algorithms, and machine learning techniques to forecast future outcomes. In the context of inventory management, it encompasses the prediction of future product demands, analysis of customer purchasing behaviors, and anticipation of market trends and fluctuations.

Key Components of Predictive Analytics in Inventory Management

- Demand Forecasting: Demand forecasting lies at the core of predictive analytics. This process involves an intricate analysis of past sales data, seasonal variations, promotional impacts, and external market dynamics. Advanced algorithms are employed to predict future product demands with remarkable precision, allowing businesses to align their inventory accordingly.

- Automated Replenishment Systems: Predictive analytics enhances inventory management by automating the replenishment process. Algorithms analyze sales velocity, lead times, and supplier performance to determine optimal reorder points, thereby maintaining adequate stock levels and reducing the risk of overstock or stock shortages.

- Price Optimization: This aspect of predictive analytics helps in formulating dynamic pricing strategies. It analyzes factors like customer demand elasticity, competitor pricing, cost variations, and market conditions to suggest optimal pricing points, thus balancing profitability with market competitiveness.

Implementing Predictive Analytics in Inventory Management

- Data Collection and Analysis: The implementation process begins with the collection of diverse data sets, including historical sales, customer transactions, market trends, and supply chain logistics. This data is then meticulously analyzed to identify patterns and derive actionable insights.

- Model Development and Training: Custom predictive models are developed, tailored to the specific needs and characteristics of the business. These models are trained on historical data, continually refined to improve their predictive accuracy.
- Integration with Inventory Systems: Seamless integration of predictive analytics tools with existing inventory management systems is essential. This integration allows for real-time data flow and decision-making, enhancing the responsiveness and agility of inventory practices.
- Continuous Monitoring and Adjustment: Predictive models require ongoing monitoring and iterative refinement to ensure they remain relevant and accurate in the face of changing market trends, consumer preferences, and supply chain dynamics.

Case Studies of Successful Implementation

Several leading e-commerce companies have successfully harnessed predictive analytics for inventory management:

- Amazon: Amazon's sophisticated inventory system employs predictive analytics to accurately forecast customer demand, central to its just-in-time inventory strategy.
- Walmart: Walmart uses predictive analytics to optimize inventory across its vast network, improving product availability while reducing waste and inefficiencies.

Challenges and Future Directions

Despite its significant advantages, predictive analytics in inventory management presents several challenges:

- Data Accuracy and Consistency: The effectiveness of predictive models is highly dependent on the accuracy, relevance, and consistency of the data used.
- Complexity in Implementation: Developing and integrating complex predictive analytics systems can be resource-intensive and require specialized expertise.
- Adaptability to Market Changes: Predictive models must be flexible and adaptive to swiftly respond to rapid changes in market conditions and consumer behavior.

The future of inventory management with predictive analytics is poised to evolve towards more sophisticated AI-driven systems, incorporating real-time analytics and deeper integration with other supply chain processes.

Conclusion

Predictive analytics is reshaping inventory management in the e-commerce industry, offering a proactive approach to anticipate and respond to future demands. This capability enhances operational efficiency, customer satisfaction, and profitability. As technology continues to advance, the role of predictive analytics in inventory management is set to become more integral, solidifying its position as a crucial tool for e-commerce businesses.

Chapter 6:
Crafting the Customer Journey: Personalization through Machine Learning

Introduction

In the highly competitive e-commerce landscape, personalization of the customer journey has transcended from being a mere luxury to a fundamental necessity. Machine Learning (ML) plays a pivotal role in this paradigm, enabling businesses to craft experiences uniquely tailored to individual customer preferences and behavior patterns. This chapter explores the multifaceted ways in which ML facilitates a customized customer journey, thereby significantly enhancing user engagement and driving sales.

The Role of Machine Learning in Personalization

- Understanding Customer Preferences: ML algorithms are adept at analyzing a plethora of customer data, encompassing past purchases, browsing history, search patterns, and even social media interactions. This analysis yields deep insights into individual preferences and behaviors, forming the bedrock of personalized customer experiences.

- Customized Product Recommendations: Arguably the most visible manifestation of ML in e-commerce, personalized product recommendations leverage sophisticated algorithms. These systems suggest products aligned with the customer's interests and past interactions, dramatically increasing the likelihood of purchase.

- Tailored Marketing Messages: Beyond product recommendations, ML significantly enhances personalized marketing efforts. This involves sending finely-tuned emails, notifications, and ads, meticulously crafted to resonate with each customer's unique interests, preferences, and purchase history.

Implementing Machine Learning for Personalization

- Data Collection and Analysis: The foundation of effective ML-driven personalization is the gathering of comprehensive and diverse customer data. This data, once collected, is analyzed to extract actionable insights and patterns.

- Developing Predictive Models: Utilizing the analyzed data, predictive models are developed to forecast customer preferences and probable future behaviors. These models integrate various ML techniques, from basic classification algorithms to more complex neural networks.

- Real-Time Adaptation: A critical aspect of ML in personalization is its ability to adapt dynamically in real-time. This means continuously updating recommendations and interactions based on the customer's ongoing activity, thereby ensuring relevance and timeliness.

- Continuous Learning and Improvement: The essence of ML lies in its capacity for continuous learning. Models evolve and refine their output over time, learning from new data and interactions, thus perpetually enhancing the personalization process.

Challenges and Ethical Considerations

Personalization via ML is not devoid of challenges:

- Privacy Concerns: In an era where data privacy is paramount, handling personal customer data demands strict compliance with data protection regulations and ethical standards.

- Balancing Personalization and Intrusiveness: Achieving the delicate balance between offering personalized experiences and avoiding perceived intrusiveness is a critical challenge.

- Data Bias: Ensuring the impartiality of data used for personalization is essential. Biased data can lead to skewed recommendations, potentially alienating customers and damaging brand reputation.

Conclusion

Machine learning has revolutionized the e-commerce sector by enabling unprecedented levels of personalization in the customer journey. As ML technologies continue to advance, the scope for more refined, nuanced, and sophisticated personalization strategies expands, heralding a future where each customer's journey is as distinctive and individualized as they are. This chapter underscores the transformative potential of ML in personalizing the e-commerce experience, highlighting its role in shaping future customer engagement strategies.

Chapter 7:
The Dynamic Pricing Ballet: Harmonizing Demand and Supply

Introduction

Dynamic pricing in e-commerce, a strategy where prices fluctuate in real-time based on market demand and supply, resembles a complex ballet. In this intricate dance, machine learning (ML) plays the role of a master choreographer, ensuring prices are fine-tuned to balance business interests and customer satisfaction. This chapter delves into the nuanced world of dynamic pricing, examining how ML orchestrates this delicate balance.

Understanding Dynamic Pricing in E-Commerce

- Demand and Supply Fluctuations: In the digital marketplace, prices are subject to rapid changes influenced by various factors such as shifts in customer demand, competitor pricing strategies, and inventory levels.

- The Role of ML in Dynamic Pricing: ML algorithms adeptly analyze these fluctuating factors to adjust prices in real-time. This continuous adjustment aims to maximize revenue while maintaining market competitiveness and customer satisfaction.

Machine Learning Techniques in Dynamic Pricing

- Predictive Analytics: Utilizing ML for predictive analytics involves forecasting future demand patterns. This foresight allows businesses to make proactive price adjustments.

- Competitor Analysis: ML algorithms can continuously monitor and analyze competitor pricing strategies. This intelligence is crucial in maintaining a competitive edge.

- Price Elasticity Modeling: A key aspect of dynamic pricing is understanding the relationship between price changes and sales volume. ML models are employed to analyze and predict this elasticity, aiding in setting prices that optimize sales and profits.

Implementing Dynamic Pricing with Machine Learning

- Data Gathering: The foundation of a robust dynamic pricing strategy is the collection of relevant data, which includes historical sales data, competitor pricing information, and current market trends.

- Model Development and Training: Developing ML models tailored to dynamic pricing involves creating algorithms that can process this data and make accurate, timely pricing decisions.

- Real-Time Pricing Adjustments: An essential feature of dynamic pricing is the ability to implement price changes in real-time, based on the model's recommendations. This requires sophisticated systems that can rapidly respond to the model's insights.

- Monitoring and Refinement: The efficacy of dynamic pricing models relies on continuous monitoring and refinement. This process ensures that the models remain accurate and effective, adapting to changing market conditions.

Challenges and Ethical Considerations

Implementing dynamic pricing through ML presents its own set of challenges:

- Customer Perception: It's crucial to manage dynamic pricing strategies in a way that does not erode customer trust or give an impression of unfairness.

- Regulatory Compliance: Businesses must ensure that their dynamic pricing strategies comply with all relevant pricing regulations, avoiding practices such as price gouging.

- Complexity in Implementation: Developing, integrating, and maintaining dynamic pricing models can be resource-intensive and require significant technical expertise.

Conclusion

The dynamic pricing strategy, orchestrated by ML, represents a sophisticated and potentially highly rewarding approach for e-commerce businesses. It allows for nimble revenue management, aligns prices with real-time market conditions, and helps maintain competitiveness. As ML technologies continue to advance, dynamic pricing strategies are poised to become even more refined and effective, further harmonizing the intricate relationship between demand and supply in the e-commerce sector. This evolution promises a future where pricing strategies are not just reactive but are proactive, insightful, and a significant contributor to business success.

Chapter 8:
Revolutionizing Warehouses: Optimization through AI

Introduction

The transformation of warehouse management is underway, largely fueled by the advancements in artificial intelligence (AI). In the e-commerce realm, where logistics play a pivotal role, AI stands as a key innovator. This chapter delves into how AI is being harnessed to revolutionize traditional warehouse operations, significantly enhancing efficiency, accuracy, and the speed of logistics processes.

The Impact of AI on Warehouse Operations

- Automated Inventory Management: AI systems have revolutionized inventory management by enabling real-time tracking and efficient management. This advancement has led to a substantial reduction in errors and a marked improvement in stock visibility and control.

- Robotics and Automation: The deployment of AI-driven robots for tasks such as picking, sorting, and moving goods has greatly accelerated warehouse operations. These robots not only speed up processes but also reduce the reliance on manual labor, leading to increased efficiency and reduced human error.

- Predictive Maintenance: Utilizing AI for predictive maintenance is a game-changer. AI algorithms are adept at predicting equipment failures before they occur, allowing for proactive maintenance. This foresight significantly reduces downtime and associated costs, maintaining a steady flow of operations.

Implementing AI in Warehouses

- Integration with Existing Systems: A crucial step in adopting AI is its integration with current warehouse management systems. This integration ensures a smooth transition and maximizes the benefits of AI technologies.

- Robotics and Automation Solutions: Implementing robotic and automated systems for repetitive and labor-intensive tasks revolutionizes warehouse operations. These systems enhance operational efficiency and accuracy while minimizing human-induced errors.

- Data Analysis for Continuous Improvement: One of the standout features of AI in warehouse management is its ability for continuous learning. AI systems constantly analyze operational data to identify areas for improvement, such as optimizing warehouse layouts or refining logistical processes.

Challenges and Considerations

- High Initial Investment: The adoption of AI and robotics in warehouse settings can be capital-intensive, requiring significant upfront investment.

- Workforce Adaptation: It's crucial to manage the transition of the existing workforce to effectively collaborate with AI systems. This transition includes training and adapting workforce skills to new technologies.

- Data Privacy and Security: With the increased use of AI, ensuring the security and privacy of the data used and generated within AI systems is paramount. This consideration is especially critical given the sensitivity of inventory and logistics data.

Conclusion

AI is rapidly establishing itself as a fundamental element in modern warehouse operations. Its ability to significantly improve efficiency, accuracy, and speed in logistics makes it an invaluable asset in the e-commerce industry. As AI technologies continue to evolve and mature, their role in enhancing and optimizing warehouse operations is set to expand, further revolutionizing the landscape of e-commerce logistics. This ongoing evolution promises a future where AI-driven warehouses are not just a possibility but a standard, marking a new era in the efficiency and effectiveness of e-commerce operations.

Chapter 9:
Navigating Success: Smart Route Optimization in Deliveries

Introduction

The efficiency of the final mile in e-commerce delivery is a critical component of customer satisfaction and operational efficiency. This chapter delves into how smart route optimization, underpinned by Artificial Intelligence (AI) and machine learning, is revolutionizing delivery logistics. It explores how these advanced technologies enable faster, more efficient, and cost-effective delivery processes.

The Role of AI in Route Optimization

- Dynamic Route Planning: AI algorithms play a crucial role in optimizing delivery routes. They analyze an array of variables including traffic patterns, delivery time windows, vehicle capacity, and geographic constraints to devise the most efficient delivery paths.

- Real-Time Adjustments: One of the standout features of AI in route optimization is its ability to adjust routes in real-time. This adaptability is key in responding to unforeseen events like traffic congestion, road closures, or last-minute delivery cancellations.

- Predictive Analytics for Planning: AI's predictive models are employed to anticipate future scenarios, such as traffic conditions and delivery volumes. This foresight allows delivery systems to proactively adjust schedules and routes, enhancing efficiency and reliability.

Implementing Smart Route Optimization

- Data Collection: The foundation of effective route optimization lies in the collection of extensive data. This data encompasses traffic patterns, weather conditions, historical delivery performance, and urban layout information.

- Algorithm Development: The heart of smart route optimization is the development of sophisticated algorithms. These algorithms must be capable of processing complex datasets and continuously learning to improve route planning efficiency.

- Integration with Delivery Systems: For route optimization to be effective, it must be seamlessly integrated with existing delivery systems. This integration ensures real-time communication and updates between the route planning tool and the delivery personnel.

Challenges and Future Directions

- Data Accuracy and Availability: The effectiveness of smart route optimization is heavily dependent on the accuracy and completeness of the underlying data. Ensuring access to reliable and comprehensive datasets is a significant challenge.

- Adapting to Rapid Changes: Delivery routes are subject to constant change due to varying traffic conditions, weather, and other unpredictable factors. The system must be agile and responsive to adapt quickly to these changes.

- Balancing Efficiency and Driver Workload: While optimizing routes for efficiency, it is also vital to consider the workload and well-being of delivery drivers. The system should balance efficient routing with realistic and manageable driver schedules.

Conclusion

Smart route optimization represents a transformative development in e-commerce delivery, significantly enhancing operational efficiency, reducing logistical costs, and improving customer satisfaction. As AI and machine learning technologies continue to advance, these route optimization systems are poised to become even more sophisticated and integral to e-commerce logistics. This evolution will further optimize the last mile of delivery, a critical component in the success and growth of e-commerce businesses.

Chapter 10:
The Reverse Flow: Refining Returns and Reverse Logistics

Introduction

The efficacy of managing returns and reverse logistics is a critical aspect of e-commerce, as important as the forward movement of goods. This chapter examines how the adoption of technology, especially machine learning (ML) and Artificial Intelligence (AI), is reshaping the handling of returns and reverse logistics. It highlights how these technological advancements can convert logistical challenges into opportunities for increased customer satisfaction and operational efficiency.

Enhancing Reverse Logistics with Technology

- Automated Returns Processing: AI-driven systems have revolutionized the processing of returns. These systems automate various aspects of the returns process, including the initiation of return requests, inspection, sorting, and restocking of returned items, making the process more efficient and less prone to error.

- Predictive Analytics for Return Reduction: ML algorithms play a significant role in analyzing return patterns. By identifying the underlying causes of returns, these algorithms enable businesses to implement proactive strategies to reduce return rates, ultimately enhancing product satisfaction and reducing logistical burdens.

- Optimization of Reverse Logistics Routes: AI technologies are also employed to optimize the collection routes for returned items. This optimization not only reduces transportation costs but also minimizes the environmental impact of reverse logistics.

Implementing Technology in Reverse Logistics

- Integrating Systems: For technology to effectively enhance reverse logistics, it must be seamlessly integrated with existing supply chain management systems. This integration ensures that data and processes flow smoothly between forward and reverse logistics operations.

- Data Analysis for Insights: Utilizing data analytics is crucial in gaining a deeper understanding of return patterns and customer behavior. This analysis can provide valuable insights, guiding the formulation of strategies to reduce returns and improve customer satisfaction.

- Enhancing Customer Experience: The application of technology in reverse logistics should aim not only at operational efficiency but also at improving the customer's experience during the return process. This includes providing easy-to-use return interfaces, transparent communication, and efficient refund or replacement processes.

Challenges and Future Directions

- Complexity in Handling Returns: Managing the myriad reasons for returns and the varying conditions of returned goods can be a complex task. Technology must be adept at handling this diversity efficiently.

- Data Privacy and Security: In the process of handling returns, ensuring the privacy and security of customer data is paramount. This is especially important as return processes often involve sensitive customer information.

- Sustainability Concerns: Another critical aspect is balancing operational efficiency with environmental sustainability. Reverse logistics should be managed in a way that minimizes environmental impact while maintaining efficiency.

Conclusion

The integration of ML and AI in reverse logistics is significantly transforming this aspect of e-commerce. By streamlining the returns process and optimizing the reverse flow of goods, businesses can not only enhance customer satisfaction but also achieve cost reductions and improve sustainability. As such, reverse logistics, powered by advanced technology, is evolving into a strategic component of the e-commerce supply chain, offering significant opportunities for business growth and customer loyalty.

Chapter 11:
Strengthening Bonds: Machine Learning in Supplier Relationship Management

Introduction

In the complex and dynamic world of e-commerce, managing supplier relationships is more than just a logistical necessity; it's a strategic imperative. This chapter explores the transformative role of machine learning (ML) in supplier relationship management (SRM), highlighting how it fortifies partnerships, streamlines communication, and enhances overall operational efficiency.

The Role of ML in Supplier Relationship Management

- Predictive Analytics for Supplier Performance: Utilizing ML for predictive analytics in SRM involves analyzing extensive supplier performance data. This analysis helps in predicting potential disruptions or issues, thereby enabling proactive management and decision-making.

- Risk Management: ML's capability in identifying and mitigating supply chain risks is invaluable. By assessing various data points, including market trends, geopolitical events, and supplier history, ML provides a nuanced understanding of potential supply chain vulnerabilities.

- Optimizing Procurement Processes: AI-driven tools are revolutionizing procurement processes. These tools automate and optimize various stages of procurement, from order placement to invoice processing and payment, thereby enhancing efficiency and reducing human error.

Implementing ML in SRM

- Data Integration: A crucial step in implementing ML in SRM is the integration of data from diverse internal and external sources. This comprehensive data amalgamation provides a holistic view of supplier relationships and supply chain dynamics.

- Developing Customized ML Models: Tailoring ML models to specific business contexts and supply chain scenarios is essential for maximizing their effectiveness. These customized models are developed to address unique challenges and objectives in supplier management.

- Collaboration Tools: Implementing AI-powered tools enhances collaboration with suppliers. These tools streamline communication, automate routine interactions, and facilitate more efficient exchange of information.

Challenges and Future Directions

- Data Quality and Integration: The accuracy and effectiveness of ML insights heavily depend on the quality and integration of data. Ensuring high-quality, cohesive data is a significant challenge in implementing ML in SRM.

- Change Management: Transitioning to AI-driven SRM systems involves significant change management. This includes training employees and suppliers to adapt to new technologies and processes.

- Balancing Technology and Human Judgment: While ML brings numerous advantages, it's crucial to maintain a balance between automated decision-making and human expertise. Human judgment remains vital in interpreting ML insights and making strategic decisions in supplier relationships.

Conclusion

Machine learning is rapidly becoming an integral component of supplier relationship management in the e-commerce sector. By offering deeper insights, predictive capabilities, and enhanced operational efficiency, ML is facilitating stronger, more collaborative, and effective supplier relationships. As ML technology continues to evolve, its role in reshaping SRM practices will become increasingly significant, marking a new era of data-driven, intelligent supplier management.

Chapter 12:
Safeguarding Transactions: ML in E-commerce Fraud Detection

Introduction

The surge in e-commerce activity has been paralleled by an increase in fraudulent activities, posing significant risks to both businesses and consumers. This chapter focuses on the application of machine learning (ML) in e-commerce fraud detection, showcasing how ML provides adaptive, intelligent, and efficient solutions to safeguard online transactions.

ML-Driven Fraud Detection Techniques

- Advanced Pattern Recognition: ML algorithms are particularly adept at discerning complex patterns in transaction data, identifying anomalies that could indicate fraudulent activities. This pattern recognition extends beyond simple rule-based systems, offering a more nuanced detection capability.

- Predictive Analytics and Risk Scoring: Utilizing historical data, ML models are capable of predicting the likelihood of fraud in transactions. These systems assign risk scores to transactions based on various indicators, effectively flagging those with a high probability of being fraudulent.

- Real-Time Transaction Analysis: The ability of ML to analyze transactions in real-time is pivotal in fraud detection. This instantaneous analysis allows for the immediate identification and prevention of fraudulent activities, significantly reducing the risk of financial loss.

Implementing ML in Fraud Detection

- Comprehensive Data Collection and Analysis: The foundation of effective ML-based fraud detection is the aggregation and analysis of extensive transaction data. This data encompasses not just the transactional details but also user behavior and interaction patterns.

- Model Development and Continuous Training: Developing ML models for fraud detection involves creating algorithms that can accurately identify fraudulent activities while minimizing false positives. These models require continuous training and updating to adapt to new fraud patterns and techniques.

- Seamless Integration with Payment Systems: For ML models to be effective in real-world scenarios, they must be seamlessly integrated with existing e-commerce payment systems. This integration ensures that fraud detection runs smoothly within the transaction process, without causing significant delays or disruptions.

Challenges and Future Outlook

- Balancing Detection Accuracy and User Experience: One of the significant challenges in ML-based fraud detection is maintaining a balance between detection accuracy and the user experience. It is crucial to minimize false positives that can inconvenience legitimate customers.

- Adapting to Evolving Fraud Techniques: As fraudsters continually refine their tactics, ML models must be agile and adaptive. Keeping these models up-to-date with the latest fraud trends is essential for maintaining effective fraud detection.

- Ensuring Data Privacy and Security: In the process of fraud detection, handling vast amounts of sensitive transaction data requires strict adherence to data privacy and security standards. It is vital to ensure that the data used in these systems is secure and protected.

Conclusion

Machine learning has emerged as a key technology in combatting e-commerce fraud, offering dynamic and sophisticated solutions to protect online transactions. As ML technologies continue to advance, their capacity for detecting and preventing fraud will become increasingly robust, addressing the evolving complexities of e-commerce fraud. This advancement not only enhances transaction security but also builds trust and reliability in the e-commerce ecosystem, benefiting both businesses and consumers alike.

Chapter 13:
Evolving Interfaces: The Adaptive Power of ML

Introduction

The interface between customers and e-commerce platforms is pivotal in shaping the online shopping experience. In this digital era, machine learning (ML) is revolutionizing these interfaces, making them more adaptive, intuitive, and personalized. This chapter explores the transformative impact of ML in enhancing e-commerce interfaces, thereby elevating the overall customer experience.

ML in Enhancing E-Commerce Interfaces

- Personalized User Experience: ML algorithms are adept at analyzing user behavior, preferences, and interaction patterns. This analysis is used to customize the browsing experience, tailoring product recommendations and content to individual users. This personalization extends to curating product displays, search results, and promotional content that align with the user's interests and behaviors.

- Chatbots and Virtual Assistants: AI-powered chatbots and virtual assistants represent a significant leap in customer service. They provide real-time, automated support, answering queries, offering product recommendations, and assisting in the purchase process. This not only enhances customer engagement but also provides 24/7 support, improving the overall service experience.

- Visual and Voice Search: Leveraging ML for advanced visual and voice search capabilities enriches the user interface. Customers can search for products using images or voice commands, making the search process more natural, convenient, and aligned with modern user habits.

Implementing Adaptive Interfaces with ML

- User Data Analysis: The effectiveness of ML-driven interfaces hinges on the collection and analysis of comprehensive user data. This includes browsing history, purchase records, search queries, and interaction metrics.

- Continuous Learning and Adaptation: ML models in e-commerce interfaces are designed to continuously learn from user interactions. This ongoing learning process allows the models to constantly improve and refine the user experience, making it more personalized and responsive over time.

- Integration with E-commerce Platforms: For ML-driven interfaces to function optimally, they need to be seamlessly integrated with the broader e-commerce platform. This integration ensures that the adaptive features are embedded within the customer's journey, from browsing to checkout.

Challenges and Considerations

- User Privacy and Trust: While personalization is beneficial, it must be balanced with user privacy concerns. Maintaining user trust is crucial, necessitating transparent data practices and adherence to privacy regulations.

- Interface Design and Usability: Designing ML-driven interfaces that are both intuitive and user-friendly is challenging. The interface should integrate advanced ML features without compromising on simplicity and ease of use.

- Technical Complexity: Developing and maintaining sophisticated ML-driven interfaces involves considerable technical complexity. It requires expertise in ML, user interface design, and software development, alongside ongoing maintenance and updates.

Conclusion

Machine learning is fundamentally reshaping the landscape of e-commerce interfaces. By rendering these interfaces more adaptive, responsive, and personalized, ML is enhancing the online shopping experience. As ML technologies continue to evolve, these interfaces are poised to become increasingly interactive and user-centric, playing a crucial role in the future of e-commerce and digital customer engagement.

Chapter 14:
The Language of Machines: NLP in E-commerce

Introduction

Natural Language Processing (NLP), a sophisticated branch of machine learning, is bringing about a paradigm shift in e-commerce communication. This chapter delves into how NLP is being harnessed in the e-commerce sector, enhancing customer interactions and providing deeper insights into consumer behavior.

NLP Applications in E-commerce

- Enhanced Customer Service: NLP is the driving force behind advanced chatbots and virtual assistants. These AI-driven tools engage customers in natural language conversations, providing instant support, answering queries, and aiding in the shopping process. This has revolutionized customer service, making it more accessible, efficient, and user-friendly.

- Sentiment Analysis: NLP's ability to analyze and interpret customer reviews and feedback is invaluable. By assessing the sentiment behind customer comments, e-commerce businesses gain critical insights into customer satisfaction and product performance, enabling them to make informed business decisions.

- Search Functionality Enhancement: NLP significantly improves e-commerce search functionalities. It enables search engines to understand and process natural language queries, leading to more accurate and relevant search results, tailored to the specific needs and preferences of users.

Implementing NLP in E-commerce

- Data Collection and Processing: Implementing NLP in e-commerce starts with the collection and processing of large datasets of textual data, including customer interactions, reviews, and queries.

- Algorithm Development and Training: Developing effective NLP algorithms involves training them to comprehend, interpret, and respond to human language accurately. This training requires a substantial dataset and involves complex algorithmic structures.

- Seamless Integration with E-commerce Systems: For NLP tools to be effective, they need to be seamlessly integrated into e-commerce platforms. This integration ensures that NLP functionalities are a coherent part of the customer's shopping experience.

Challenges and Opportunities

- Language Diversity and Complexity: NLP faces the challenge of dealing with the diverse and complex nature of human language, including idioms, slang, and varying dialects.

- Continuous Learning and Improvement: NLP models require ongoing training and updates to adapt to new languages, evolving language use, and the introduction of new products and services.

- Balancing Automation and Human Touch: While NLP offers numerous advantages in automating customer service, it's crucial to balance this automation with the human elements of customer interaction, ensuring that customer service remains empathetic and personal.

Conclusion

NLP is significantly transforming the interaction landscape in e-commerce, offering more intuitive, efficient, and customer-centric communication methods. As NLP technology continues to advance, its application in e-commerce is expected to broaden, enhancing customer experiences and providing deeper business insights. This ongoing evolution of NLP will continue to shape the future of e-commerce, making interactions more human-like and insightful, and thus driving customer engagement and business growth.

Chapter 15:
Seeing the Unseen: Visual Recognition Technologies in E-commerce

Introduction

In the digital era, visual recognition technologies, powered by advanced machine learning (ML), are revolutionizing the e-commerce landscape. This chapter delves into the transformative role of these technologies in enhancing online shopping experiences, improving product discovery, and streamlining e-commerce operations, thereby forging a new paradigm in digital retail.

Applications of Visual Recognition in E-commerce

- Image-Based Search: Visual recognition enables customers to search for products using images. This groundbreaking approach transcends traditional keyword-based searches, offering a more intuitive and user-friendly shopping experience. Customers can simply upload an image of the desired product, and the system will present similar or matching items from the e-commerce catalog.

- Product Tagging and Categorization: Automating product tagging and categorization using visual recognition technologies significantly improves the efficiency and accuracy of e-commerce catalogs. This technology can quickly analyze product images, identify features, and categorize items based on visual characteristics, thereby enhancing the accuracy of product listings and search results.

- Quality Control: Visual recognition is increasingly employed for quality control purposes. By analyzing product images, these systems can detect defects, inconsistencies, and deviations from quality standards, ensuring that only products meeting the required criteria reach the consumer.

Implementing Visual Recognition Technologies

- Developing and Training ML Models: The core of visual recognition in e-commerce lies in developing robust ML models capable of accurately interpreting visual data. These models are trained on extensive datasets of product images and user interactions to enhance their accuracy and reliability.

- Integration with E-commerce Platforms: For visual recognition technologies to be effective, they must be seamlessly integrated into existing e-commerce platforms. This integration ensures that visual search and categorization features are easily accessible to customers and are harmoniously woven into the overall shopping experience.

- Ensuring Data Privacy and Security: In deploying visual recognition technologies, safeguarding user data privacy and security is paramount. E-commerce platforms must implement stringent data protection measures to secure the images and information provided by users.

Challenges and Future Outlook

- Technical Complexity: Developing visual recognition models that are both accurate and efficient requires significant technical expertise and resources. The complexity lies in processing diverse and vast datasets and ensuring the models are adaptable to various product categories.

- Data Diversity and Inclusivity: Training visual recognition models on diverse and inclusive data sets is crucial to ensure they recognize a broad range of products and cater to a diverse customer base.

- Balancing Automation and Human Oversight: While automation enhances operational efficiency, maintaining a balance with human oversight is essential, particularly in areas like quality control, to ensure the accuracy and reliability of automated systems.

Conclusion

Visual recognition technology is reshaping e-commerce, offering innovative and efficient ways to interact with customers and manage products. As these technologies continue to evolve, their applications in e-commerce are expected to become more comprehensive and sophisticated, significantly enhancing both the customer experience and operational efficiency in digital retail.

Chapter 16:
Green Innovation: Machine Learning in Sustainable Packaging

Introduction

Sustainability is increasingly at the forefront of e-commerce, with a particular focus on packaging. This chapter explores the innovative application of machine learning (ML) in developing sustainable packaging solutions, aiming to reduce environmental impact while maintaining operational efficiency and meeting customer expectations.

ML in Sustainable Packaging

- Optimizing Packaging Design: ML algorithms are instrumental in designing environmentally friendly packaging. By analyzing factors such as product size, shape, and fragility, ML models can suggest packaging designs that minimize material use without compromising product protection.

- Predictive Analytics for Packaging Needs: Utilizing ML for predictive analytics in packaging involves forecasting the most suitable packaging options for various products and orders. This approach aims to minimize waste by tailoring packaging to the specific needs of each item, thereby reducing excess material use.

- Innovation in Sustainable Materials: ML aids in the research and development of new sustainable packaging materials. By analyzing material properties, environmental impact, and production processes, ML models can help identify materials that are both eco-friendly and practical for packaging purposes.

Implementing ML for Sustainable Packaging

- Data Collection and Analysis: Implementing ML in sustainable packaging begins with collecting and analyzing data related to current packaging practices, materials, and their environmental impact. This data provides the foundation for developing predictive models.

- Development of Predictive Models: Creating ML models that can accurately predict the most efficient and sustainable packaging solutions is a key component of this initiative. These models are trained on diverse datasets to ensure they can accommodate a wide range of packaging scenarios.

- Collaboration with Experts: Effective implementation of sustainable packaging solutions involves collaboration with material scientists, environmental experts, and suppliers. This collaborative approach is essential for developing and sourcing innovative and sustainable packaging materials.

Challenges and Opportunities

- Balancing Sustainability with Practicality: One of the main challenges in sustainable packaging is finding solutions that are both environmentally friendly and practically feasible in terms of protection, cost, and production.

- Integration into Existing Supply Chains: Incorporating sustainable packaging solutions into existing e-commerce supply chains can be complex, requiring adjustments in logistics, storage, and handling processes.

- Consumer Acceptance and Education: Educating consumers about the benefits and necessity of sustainable packaging is crucial for widespread acceptance. E-commerce platforms must communicate the value of these initiatives to foster consumer support and participation.

Conclusion

Machine learning is playing a pivotal role in advancing sustainable packaging solutions in e-commerce. By optimizing packaging designs and promoting the use of eco-friendly materials, ML is helping to reduce the environmental footprint of e-commerce operations. This aligns with the growing consumer demand for sustainability and represents a significant step toward more environmentally responsible e-commerce practices.

Chapter 17:
Bracing for the Unknown: ML in E-commerce Disaster Recovery

Introduction

In the volatile realm of e-commerce, disaster recovery is not just a contingency plan; it is an essential aspect of maintaining business continuity in the face of unpredictable challenges. This chapter examines the integral role of machine learning (ML) in enhancing e-commerce disaster recovery strategies, highlighting how it equips businesses to adapt and recover swiftly from unforeseen disruptions.

ML in E-commerce Disaster Recovery

- Predictive Analytics for Risk Assessment: ML excels in analyzing extensive datasets to forecast potential risks and prepare for various disaster scenarios. These predictive models, trained on historical data, can anticipate disruptions ranging from cyberattacks to supply chain breakdowns, enabling businesses to formulate preemptive strategies and response plans.

- Automating Recovery Processes: ML aids in automating critical aspects of the disaster recovery process. This automation includes triggering immediate response protocols, coordinating recovery tasks, and allocating resources efficiently, thereby reducing response times and mitigating the impact of disruptions.

- Optimized Data Backup and Recovery: In e-commerce, where data is a critical asset, ML algorithms optimize backup processes and facilitate rapid data recovery post-disaster. By prioritizing data based on its relevance and importance, these systems ensure that vital information is backed up more frequently and recovered swiftly, minimizing operational downtime.

Implementing ML in Disaster Recovery

- Developing Robust ML Models: The foundation of utilizing ML in disaster recovery lies in developing robust models that can accurately predict risks and streamline recovery operations. These models are trained on diverse datasets, encompassing a variety of disaster scenarios and recovery protocols.

- Integration with Disaster Recovery Plans: Effective ML implementation requires integration into broader disaster recovery and business continuity plans. This ensures that ML-driven processes are harmonized with overall business strategies, allowing for coordinated and effective disaster response.

- Regular Testing and Upgrading: To maintain their efficacy, ML models must be regularly tested and updated. This continuous improvement process is crucial for adapting to emerging risks and evolving disaster recovery requirements.

Challenges and Future Directions

- Predicting Unpredictable Events: The unpredictable nature of disasters presents a significant challenge to ML models. Developing models that can anticipate a wide range of scenarios, including rare or unprecedented events, is crucial.

- Ensuring Data Security and Privacy: Protecting sensitive data during automated backup and recovery processes is imperative. Implementing robust cybersecurity measures is essential to safeguard data integrity and privacy.

- Resource Allocation and Management: Balancing resource allocation between disaster recovery and other business priorities is critical. Strategic investments in ML-driven disaster recovery must be considered within the broader context of business operations and growth.

- Future Directions: Looking ahead, ML in disaster recovery is set to evolve with advancements in AI and data analytics. Integration with emerging technologies like blockchain for secure data management and the Internet of Things (IoT) for real-time monitoring and response will further enhance disaster recovery strategies.

Conclusion

Machine learning has become an indispensable tool in e-commerce disaster recovery, providing businesses with advanced capabilities to predict, prepare, and respond to various disruptions. As ML technology continues to evolve, its role in fortifying the resilience of e-commerce operations against the unknown is set to expand, ensuring that businesses can navigate uncertainties more effectively and maintain continuity in the face of adversity.

Chapter 18:
The Green Leap: Towards Sustainable and Eco-Friendly Logistics

Introduction

The e-commerce industry, growing exponentially, faces a significant challenge in balancing its expansion with environmental sustainability. This chapter delves into how technological advancements, especially machine learning (ML), are empowering e-commerce logistics to become more sustainable and eco-friendly. It explores the innovative approaches being adopted in the sector to minimize environmental impact while maintaining efficiency and customer satisfaction.

Sustainable Practices in E-Commerce Logistics

- Eco-friendly Transportation Solutions: A pivotal area where ML is making an impact is in the optimization of delivery routes. These advanced algorithms analyze vast amounts of data on traffic patterns, weather conditions, and delivery schedules to determine the most efficient routes, thereby reducing fuel consumption and emissions. Additionally, ML is facilitating the transition to electric and hybrid delivery vehicles by optimizing their routes and charging schedules.

- Revolutionizing Packaging: ML is being employed to revolutionize packaging processes. By analyzing product dimensions, shipping distances, and durability requirements, ML algorithms can determine the minimum necessary packaging, significantly reducing material waste. Furthermore, these algorithms are instrumental in the adoption of biodegradable and recyclable materials, ensuring that packaging is not only efficient but also environmentally responsible.

- Energy-Efficient Warehousing: AI and ML are transforming warehousing operations by optimizing energy consumption. This includes intelligent lighting systems, temperature controls, and automation of energy-intensive processes. By analyzing usage patterns and external factors like weather, ML models can adjust operations in real-time to minimize energy use while maintaining operational efficiency.

Implementing Sustainable Logistics

- Data-Driven Insights for Green Initiatives: Implementing sustainable logistics begins with data. By harnessing data analytics, businesses can gain insights into their operations' environmental impact, identify areas for improvement, and track the effectiveness of implemented sustainability measures.

- Building Collaborative Eco-Conscious Networks: Establishing partnerships with suppliers, logistics providers, and other stakeholders committed to sustainability is essential. These collaborations can lead to shared sustainability goals, pooled resources for eco-friendly initiatives, and a unified approach to green logistics.

- Customer Engagement in Sustainability: Transparent communication about sustainability efforts and actively involving customers in these initiatives can enhance brand loyalty and consumer trust. E-commerce platforms can educate customers about their sustainable practices and offer eco-friendly choices, such as green shipping options or sustainable product lines.

Challenges and Future Directions

- Cost-Sustainability Balance: A primary challenge is the balance between cost and sustainability. Green logistics often require initial investments and can alter operational costs, requiring a strategic approach to ensure profitability.

- Adapting to Technological Advances: Keeping pace with rapid technological advancements and integrating them seamlessly into existing logistics frameworks is critical. This requires continuous investment in new technologies and training for staff.

- Navigating Regulatory Landscapes: As environmental regulations evolve, staying compliant is crucial. E-commerce businesses must be agile in adapting to new standards and proactive in implementing practices that meet or exceed regulatory requirements.

Conclusion

The shift towards sustainable and eco-friendly logistics, driven by machine learning and other technological innovations, is a significant and necessary step for the e-commerce industry. This green leap not only addresses pressing environmental concerns but also opens avenues for innovation, efficiency, and enhanced customer engagement. As technology continues to evolve, the potential for creating an even more sustainable e-commerce logistics network grows, promising a future where the digital marketplace thrives in harmony with the environment.

Chapter 19:
Ethics in the Algorithm: Navigating ML's Moral Landscape in E-commerce

Introduction

The integration of machine learning (ML) in e-commerce is a leap forward in technological innovation, but it brings with it a complex web of ethical considerations. This chapter delves into the moral landscape of ML in e-commerce, examining the ethical implications of its application and the imperative of responsible AI practices. It discusses the challenges and responsibilities of integrating ML ethically into e-commerce systems.

Ethical Considerations in ML

- Data Privacy and Security: At the forefront of ethical considerations is the handling of customer data. ML in e-commerce must respect privacy rights and implement robust security measures to protect data against breaches. Ethical handling involves transparency in data collection, usage, and storage, along with stringent measures to safeguard data integrity.

- Bias and Fairness: ML algorithms, based on the data they are trained on, can inadvertently perpetuate biases, leading to unfair treatment of certain customer groups or suppliers. It is crucial to address these biases by ensuring algorithms are fair and impartial, providing equal treatment to all users.

- Transparency and Accountability: There is a growing need for transparency in ML decision-making processes. Users should be able to understand how and why certain algorithmic decisions are made. Additionally, there must be accountability mechanisms in place for the outcomes of these decisions, particularly in cases where they impact consumer rights or well-being.

Implementing Ethical ML Practices

- Ethical Frameworks and Guidelines: Establishing ethical frameworks and guidelines for ML usage in e-commerce is essential. These frameworks should govern the development and application of ML technologies, ensuring they align with broader ethical principles and societal values.

- Diverse and Inclusive Data Sets: To reduce the risk of inherent biases in ML models, it's important to use diverse and inclusive datasets in their training. This involves gathering data that accurately represents different demographics and consumer groups.

- Regular Audits and Reviews: Conducting regular audits and reviews of ML algorithms is essential to ensure ongoing ethical compliance. These audits can help identify any emerging biases or ethical issues and provide opportunities to rectify them promptly.

Challenges and Future Outlook

- Keeping Pace with Technological Advancements: As ML technology rapidly evolves, ethical considerations must evolve alongside it. Staying abreast of the latest developments and understanding their ethical implications is crucial.

- Balancing Innovation and Ethics: E-commerce businesses face the challenge of leveraging ML for growth and innovation while adhering to ethical practices. Finding this balance is key to sustainable and responsible business practices.

- Global Standards and Regulations: Navigating the complex and often varied landscape of global standards and regulations related to AI and data privacy is another significant challenge. E-commerce platforms operating internationally must be compliant across different legal jurisdictions.

Conclusion

As ML technology continues to reshape the e-commerce sector, ethical considerations will increasingly influence how this technology is developed, implemented, and used. Navigating the moral landscape of ML is not only crucial for maintaining consumer trust and platform integrity but also for ensuring that technological advancements contribute positively to society. As we move forward, ethical considerations in ML will remain a pivotal aspect, guiding the responsible and equitable use of AI in e-commerce.

Chapter 20:
Synchronized Intelligence: Integrating ML and IoT in Supply Chain Monitoring

Introduction

The integration of Machine Learning (ML) with the Internet of Things (IoT) is heralding a transformative era in supply chain monitoring, especially within the e-commerce sector. This synergistic combination of technologies offers unprecedented efficiency and insight, reshaping how supply chains are managed and optimized. This chapter delves into how ML and IoT, working in tandem, are revolutionizing supply chain operations, enhancing real-time tracking, predictive analytics, and inventory management.

ML and IoT in Supply Chain Monitoring

- Real-Time Tracking and Monitoring: The deployment of IoT devices across the supply chain provides a continuous stream of real-time data on the movement and condition of goods. When coupled with ML algorithms, this data can be analyzed to optimize routes, predict potential delays, and enhance the efficiency of logistics processes. This integration results in a more transparent, responsive, and reliable supply chain.

- Predictive Maintenance and Equipment Management: IoT sensors on equipment and vehicles collect vast amounts of operational data. ML algorithms process this data to predict potential failures and schedule maintenance proactively. This predictive maintenance approach minimizes downtime, extends the life of equipment, and ensures uninterrupted supply chain operations.

- Enhanced Inventory Management and Demand Forecasting: Integrating IoT with ML-driven inventory management systems revolutionizes stock monitoring. IoT sensors provide real-time data on inventory levels, while ML models analyze this data alongside market trends and consumer behavior for accurate demand forecasting. This synergy results in optimal stock levels, reduced waste, and more efficient inventory management.

Implementing ML and IoT Integration

- Strategic Deployment of IoT Devices: Implementing this integrated approach begins with strategically deploying IoT sensors and devices throughout the supply chain – in warehouses, on transport vehicles, and within products. This deployment must be planned to ensure comprehensive coverage and data collection.

- Developing Advanced ML Algorithms: The next step involves developing advanced ML algorithms capable of processing the massive influx of data from IoT devices. These algorithms must be tailored to identify patterns, predict trends, and generate actionable insights from real-time data.

- Seamless System Integration and Interoperability: For maximum effectiveness, ML and IoT systems must be seamlessly integrated into the existing supply chain infrastructure. This integration should ensure interoperability between different systems and devices, facilitating smooth data flow and utilization.

Challenges and Opportunities

- Complex Data Management and Analytics: One of the primary challenges in this integration is the management and analysis of large volumes of data generated by IoT devices. This requires robust data processing infrastructure and sophisticated analytics capabilities.

- Infrastructure Investment and Scalability: Significant investment in infrastructure is required to support the integration of ML and IoT. This includes not only the initial deployment of IoT devices but also the scaling of ML systems to handle increasing data volumes.

- Cybersecurity and Data Privacy: With the increased use of IoT devices and data analytics, ensuring cybersecurity and data privacy is paramount. Safeguarding against data breaches and unauthorized access is crucial for maintaining the integrity and confidentiality of supply chain information.

Conclusion

The integration of ML and IoT in supply chain monitoring is a game-changing development in the realm of e-commerce. This synchronized intelligence not only streamlines operational processes but also provides critical insights for decision-making, offering a substantial competitive advantage. As these technologies continue to evolve, their role in enhancing supply chain efficiency and responsiveness is set to grow, marking a new chapter in the evolution of e-commerce logistics.

Chapter 21:
Quantum Horizons: The Future of E-commerce Logistics

Introduction

In the book "The Dance of Data and Delivery: Choreographing E-commerce Supply Chains through Machine Learning," we've explored the intricate interplay of data and machine learning in reshaping e-commerce logistics. As we look to the future, the advent of quantum computing presents a new horizon, promising to revolutionize the logistics landscape. This article, "Quantum Horizons: The Future of E-commerce Logistics," delves into the transformative potential of quantum computing in e-commerce logistics.

Quantum Computing: An Overview

Definition and Basic Principles

- The Concept of Quantum Computing: Quantum computing represents a paradigm shift in data processing, utilizing the principles of quantum mechanics. Unlike classical computing, which relies on bits that represent either a 0 or a 1, quantum computing uses quantum bits or qubits. These qubits can exist in a state of superposition, embodying multiple states (0 and 1) simultaneously.

- Superposition and Entanglement: Two fundamental principles of quantum mechanics that quantum computing harnesses are superposition and entanglement. Superposition allows qubits to perform multiple calculations at once, while entanglement enables qubits at different locations to be correlated in a way that changes to one affect the other, regardless of distance.

Advantages Over Classical Computing

- Parallelism and Speed: The ability of qubits to exist in multiple states enables quantum computers to perform many calculations simultaneously, offering a dramatic increase in processing speed over classical computers.

- Handling Complex Systems: Quantum computing is particularly adept at solving problems involving vast datasets and highly complex algorithms, which are common in logistics and supply chain optimization.

Quantum Computing in E-commerce Logistics

Route Optimization

- Advanced Route Calculations: Quantum computers can analyze and optimize delivery routes by processing countless variables in real-time, from traffic patterns to weather conditions and delivery windows, ensuring the most efficient routes are chosen.

- Dynamic Routing: The ability to dynamically reroute based on real-time data can lead to significant reductions in delivery times and costs, enhancing customer satisfaction and operational efficiency.

Inventory Management

- Predictive Demand Forecasting: Quantum computing can sift through complex patterns in historical sales data, seasonal trends, and market analysis to predict future demand with high precision, allowing for more accurate inventory planning.

- Responsive Replenishment Strategies: It facilitates responsive and automated replenishment systems, reducing the risks of overstocking and stockouts, and optimizing storage and warehousing costs.

Supply Chain Resilience

- Scenario Analysis: Quantum computing's ability to quickly evaluate multiple supply chain scenarios enables businesses to better prepare for potential disruptions, from supplier issues to global events like pandemics.

- Real-time Decision Making: The speed at which quantum computers process information allows for real-time decision-making in crisis situations, enhancing the resilience and adaptability of supply chains.

Quantum computing offers transformative potential for e-commerce logistics, bringing unprecedented computational power to tackle complex logistics optimization challenges. Its ability to process vast amounts of data at incredible speeds makes it an invaluable tool for route optimization, inventory management, and enhancing supply chain resilience. As quantum computing technology continues to evolve, its integration into e-commerce logistics will likely redefine the efficiency and responsiveness of supply chains, setting new benchmarks in operational excellence.

Integrating Quantum Computing with Machine Learning

Enhanced Data Analysis

- Expediting Complex Computations: Quantum computing's ability to handle complex computations at unprecedented speeds can significantly enhance the data analysis capabilities of machine learning algorithms. This synergy can lead to more sophisticated data models that can uncover deeper insights.

- Handling High-Dimensional Data: In e-commerce logistics, where data is often high-dimensional and vast, quantum computing can empower machine learning models to process and analyze this data more efficiently, leading to more accurate predictive models for customer behavior, demand forecasting, and supply chain optimization.

Real-time Decision Making

- Dynamic Pricing Models: Quantum computing enables machine learning algorithms to analyze market conditions, consumer behavior, and inventory levels in real-time to adjust pricing dynamically, enhancing profitability and market responsiveness.

- Adaptive Logistics: The integration of quantum computing with machine learning can result in highly adaptive logistics systems. These systems can instantaneously reroute shipments, adjust to unforeseen delays, and optimize delivery schedules as conditions change.

Challenges and Future Prospects

Technological Challenges

- Quantum Hardware Development: One of the primary challenges is developing stable and scalable quantum computers. Issues such as qubit coherence, error rates, and the physical size of quantum computers need addressing.

- Quantum Algorithm Development: Creating algorithms specifically designed for quantum computing is another hurdle. These algorithms need to be tailored to leverage the unique properties of quantum mechanics and are fundamentally different from classical algorithms.

Integration with Existing Systems

- Systems Architecture and Compatibility: Integrating quantum computing with existing e-commerce logistics systems requires rethinking current IT architecture. The challenge lies in ensuring compatibility between quantum computing processes and classical computing systems.

- Data Integration: The process of integrating data from existing e-commerce platforms into quantum-ready formats poses significant challenges, requiring new data management strategies and tools.

Future Prospects

- Advancements in Quantum Technologies: As research and development in quantum computing continue, we can expect breakthroughs in hardware stability, algorithm efficiency, and integration methods.

- Potential Applications in E-commerce: Future advancements may lead to widespread adoption of quantum computing in various aspects of e-commerce logistics, such as more accurate demand prediction models, AI-driven customer service chatbots, and highly efficient global supply chain management.

- Collaboration and Innovation: Collaborations between tech companies, academic institutions, and logistics businesses are likely to drive innovations in this space, leading to practical applications of quantum computing in e-commerce logistics.

In summary, the integration of quantum computing with machine learning presents a promising frontier for revolutionizing e-commerce logistics. While there are significant challenges to overcome, particularly in technology development and integration, the potential benefits in enhanced data analysis and real-time decision-making are immense. As we move forward, continued advancements in quantum computing will likely open new avenues for optimizing and transforming e-commerce supply chains.

The Road Ahead: Preparing for Quantum Integration

Investment in Research and Development

- Strategic Partnerships: Encouraging collaborations between e-commerce companies, quantum computing startups, and academic institutions to drive innovation. These partnerships can lead to the development of tailored quantum algorithms and solutions specifically for logistics and supply chain challenges.

- Funding and Support: Allocating financial resources to support quantum computing initiatives. This includes funding for startups specializing in quantum computing, grants for academic research, and investment in in-house quantum research labs.

- Focus on Practical Applications: Directing R&D efforts towards practical applications of quantum computing in e-commerce logistics, such as complex optimization problems, to create tangible improvements in supply chain efficiency and accuracy.

Training and Skill Development

- Educational Programs and Workshops: Developing educational programs and workshops focused on quantum computing and its applications in e-commerce logistics. This can involve partnerships with educational institutions or internal training programs to build a quantum-savvy workforce.

- Cross-disciplinary Learning: Encouraging cross-disciplinary learning where logistics professionals gain insights into quantum computing, and quantum scientists understand the unique challenges and needs of the e-commerce logistics sector.

- Certifications and Specializations: Offering certifications and specialized courses in quantum computing for logistics, which can help professionals in the field stay ahead of the curve in terms of emerging technologies.

Building a Quantum-Ready Infrastructure

- Upgrading IT Systems: Preparing for quantum integration by upgrading existing IT infrastructure to be compatible with quantum computing technologies. This involves assessing current systems and determining what changes are necessary to support quantum processes.

- Quantum-Safe Cybersecurity: As quantum computing has the potential to break traditional encryption methods, investing in quantum-safe cybersecurity measures is essential. This includes developing new encryption algorithms that can withstand quantum computing capabilities.

Creating a Quantum-Inclusive Business Culture

- Promoting Quantum Awareness: Building awareness of quantum computing within the organization, highlighting its potential impact and opportunities. This could involve regular knowledge-sharing sessions, seminars, and collaboration with quantum experts.

- Adaptive Business Strategies: Developing business strategies that are adaptive to the integration of quantum computing. This includes scenario planning and developing flexible business models that can quickly leverage quantum computing advancements as they become available.

Conclusion

Quantum computing stands on the horizon of e-commerce logistics, poised to bring about transformative changes. Its potential to dramatically improve route optimization, inventory management, and overall supply chain resilience could redefine the efficiency and responsiveness of e-commerce operations. However, harnessing this potential will require overcoming significant technological challenges and rethinking existing infrastructure. As we venture into this quantum future, the intersection of quantum computing and machine learning will undoubtedly play a pivotal role in choreographing the next generation of e-commerce supply chains, making them more intelligent, efficient, and adaptable to the ever-evolving market demands.

Chapter 22:
Harmonizing Tomorrow: Visioning the Next Era of E-commerce Supply Chains

Introduction

In the rapidly evolving domain of e-commerce, the fusion of machine learning and supply chain management is not just an innovation; it's a revolution. "The Dance of Data and Delivery: Choreographing E-commerce Supply Chains through Machine Learning" encapsulates this transformation. This article, "Harmonizing Tomorrow: Visioning the Next Era of E-commerce Supply Chains," aims to provide a forward-looking perspective on how this synergy will continue to evolve and shape the future of e-commerce logistics.

The Evolution of E-commerce Supply Chains

Past to Present

- Traditional Models to Technological Integration: The journey from the early days of manual inventory systems and paper-based tracking to digitalization. Discussing how innovations like the barcode and electronic data interchange (EDI) laid the groundwork for more advanced technologies in supply chains.

- The Rise of E-commerce: Exploring the advent of e-commerce in the late 20th century and how it necessitated rapid developments in supply chain management, with a focus on speed, efficiency, and scalability.

- Advancements in Technology: Detailing how the rise of cloud computing, big data analytics, and mobile technologies has revolutionized procurement, inventory management, and delivery processes, leading to more agile and responsive supply chains.

Current Trends

- Integration of Machine Learning: Delving into the current state of machine learning in supply chains, including how algorithms analyze data for better demand forecasting, inventory optimization, and efficient route planning.

- AI-Driven Customer Service: Discussing the transformation in customer service, where AI and chatbots provide personalized customer interactions, automated responses, and 24/7 service, enhancing the overall customer experience.

Emerging Technologies and Their Impact

Blockchain for Enhanced Transparency

- Trust and Traceability: Exploring how blockchain's decentralized and immutable ledger provides a new level of trust and transparency in e-commerce supply chains, making it easier to verify the authenticity of products and track their journey from manufacturer to consumer.

- Smart Contracts: Discussing the use of blockchain smart contracts in automating and streamlining supply chain agreements and payments, reducing the need for intermediaries and enhancing efficiency.

IoT and Real-Time Data

- Enhanced Tracking and Monitoring: Detailing how IoT devices, such as sensors and RFID tags, provide real-time data on product location, condition, and environmental factors, enabling more effective tracking and management of goods.

- Predictive Maintenance and Inventory Management: Explaining how IoT facilitates predictive maintenance of equipment, reducing downtimes, and IoT-based inventory management systems that automatically adjust stock levels, leading to more efficient operations.

The evolution of e-commerce supply chains is marked by significant technological advancements, transitioning from traditional methods to sophisticated, data-driven models powered by AI and machine learning. Emerging technologies like blockchain and IoT are further enhancing transparency, security, and operational efficiency in these supply chains. As these technologies continue to mature and integrate, they promise to drive the e-commerce logistics industry towards greater innovation and effectiveness.

The Role of Machine Learning in Future E-commerce Logistics

Predictive and Prescriptive Analytics

- Evolution of Analytics: Detailing the progression from predictive analytics, which forecasts future trends based on historical data, to prescriptive analytics, which suggests actions to achieve desired outcomes. This evolution marks a significant shift from reactive to proactive supply chain management.

- Scenario Planning and Risk Mitigation: Exploring how machine learning will enhance scenario planning, enabling businesses to simulate various supply chain disruptions and develop strategies to mitigate risks effectively.

Personalization at Scale

- Customized Consumer Experiences: Examining how machine learning enables the creation of highly personalized shopping experiences, by analyzing individual consumer data and preferences, leading to tailored product recommendations and personalized marketing.

- Optimized Delivery Systems: Discussing the role of machine learning in customizing delivery schedules and routes based on customer preferences and real-time data, improving customer satisfaction and operational efficiency.

Integrating Sustainability in Supply Chains

Eco-friendly Logistics

- Green Transportation Methods: Analyzing the shift towards more sustainable logistics, including the use of electric vehicles, biofuels, and optimizing delivery routes for reduced carbon emissions.

- Sustainable Packaging Solutions: Exploring the adoption of eco-friendly packaging materials and the use of machine learning to optimize packaging design for minimal waste and increased efficiency.

Circular Economy Models

- Machine Learning in Resource Optimization: Highlighting how machine learning algorithms can be pivotal in resource optimization, waste reduction, and promoting the reuse and recycling of materials, essential elements of the circular economy.

- Supply Chain Sustainability Analytics: Discussing the use of machine learning to analyze and improve the overall sustainability footprint of supply chain operations, from raw material sourcing to end-of-life product management.

Overcoming Challenges and Preparing for the Future

Adapting to Rapid Technological Changes

- Agile Adaptation Strategies: Addressing the necessity for supply chain systems to remain agile and adaptable to integrate emerging technologies swiftly.

- Continuous Technological Evaluation: Emphasizing the importance of continually evaluating and testing new technologies to determine their applicability and effectiveness in enhancing supply chain operations.

Workforce Development and Skill Upgradation

- Skill Development Programs: Discussing the development of specialized training programs and workshops to upskill the workforce in areas such as data analytics, machine learning, and sustainable supply chain management.

- Collaboration with Educational Institutions: Suggesting partnerships with universities and educational institutions to develop curriculum and courses that are in line with the evolving needs of the e-commerce logistics sector.

The future of e-commerce logistics, heavily influenced by machine learning, holds immense potential for advanced analytics, personalization, and sustainability. However, realizing this potential requires overcoming challenges related to the rapid pace of technological change and the continuous development of the workforce. By embracing these advancements and preparing for future trends, e-commerce logistics can harmonize efficiency with innovation, leading to more responsive, customer-centric, and sustainable supply chain models.

Conclusion

As we look towards the next era of e-commerce supply chains, it is clear that the integration of machine learning will continue to be a key driver of innovation and efficiency. The future will see more advanced technologies like blockchain, IoT, and AI not only optimizing operations but also embedding sustainability into the core of e-commerce logistics. However, navigating this future will require overcoming significant challenges, including the rapid pace of technological change and the need for continuous workforce development. By embracing these changes and preparing for the emerging trends, e-commerce businesses can harmonize their operations with the evolving landscape, ensuring they not only survive but thrive in the next era of e-commerce supply chains. The dance of data and delivery, choreographed by machine learning, is poised to lead e-commerce logistics into a more efficient, personalized, and sustainable future.

Appendix A:
Lexicon Unveiled: Key Terms in ML-Driven Supply Chains

For professionals in the rapidly evolving domain of e-commerce, a clear understanding of the terminology related to machine learning (ML) and supply chain management is vital. This appendix aims to demystify the jargon and elucidate key terms and concepts pertinent to ML-driven supply chains. It serves as an essential glossary, providing clarity and insight into the language commonly used in this innovative field.

Key Terms and Concepts

- Algorithm: In the context of AI and ML, an algorithm is a complex set of rules and instructions designed to guide systems in learning from data and making decisions based on that learning.

- Artificial Intelligence (AI): This broad area of computer science is focused on creating intelligent machines capable of performing tasks that typically require human intelligence, including problem-solving, learning, and decision-making.

- Big Data: Refers to extraordinarily large datasets, which can be computationally analyzed to uncover patterns, trends, and associations, particularly those relating to human behavior and interactions.

- Blockchain: A digital ledger system known for its security and transparency. In supply chains, blockchain technology is employed to enhance the traceability and integrity of transactions and product flows.

- Chatbot: Software applications that simulate human conversation, either through text or voice interactions. Often powered by NLP, chatbots are increasingly used in customer service and support.

- Data Mining: The practice of examining large datasets to discover patterns and relationships that can inform business decisions and strategies.

- Demand Forecasting: Involves predicting future customer demand for products or services using historical data, market trends, and statistical models.

- E-commerce Logistics: Encompasses the range of activities involved in storing, handling, and transporting goods sold online, including warehousing, order fulfillment, and delivery operations.

- Internet of Things (IoT): Refers to a network of interconnected devices embedded with sensors, software, and other technologies. These devices collect and exchange data, enabling enhanced automation and insights in various applications, including supply chain monitoring.

- Machine Learning (ML): A subset of AI, ML involves developing algorithms that can learn and adapt independently by analyzing and processing data, improving their performance over time without human intervention.

- Natural Language Processing (NLP): A branch of AI that enables computers to understand, interpret, and respond to human language in a useful way. NLP is key in developing tools like chatbots and voice assistants.

- Predictive Analytics: Uses historical data, along with statistical algorithms and ML techniques, to forecast future events or trends. In supply chains, predictive analytics can be used for demand forecasting, risk management, and optimization.

- Real-time Data Processing: The capability to process and analyze data immediately as it becomes available. This enables businesses to make decisions and respond to situations in real-time, a crucial aspect of modern supply chain management.

- Supply Chain Automation: The use of various technologies to streamline and optimize the processes within a supply chain. Automation can enhance efficiency, reduce errors, and lower operational costs.

- Supply Chain Management (SCM): Involves overseeing and managing the entire production flow of a product or service, from the initial sourcing of raw materials to the delivery of the final product to the consumer.

- Sustainable Supply Chain: A supply chain management approach that integrates environmental and social considerations into the lifecycle of a supply chain. This approach aims to minimize environmental impact and promote ethical practices.

This lexicon provides a foundational understanding of the key terms frequently encountered in discussions surrounding ML-driven supply chains, particularly in the e-commerce context. It serves as a valuable resource for professionals, students, and enthusiasts, helping to navigate the complex terminology of this innovative and rapidly evolving field.

Appendix B:
Regulatory Landscapes: Compliance in AI-Enhanced E-commerce

In the rapidly evolving field of AI-enhanced e-commerce, understanding and adhering to various regulatory frameworks is crucial for businesses. This appendix offers a comprehensive overview of the key regulations, guidelines, and ethical considerations that e-commerce businesses employing AI and ML technologies must navigate to ensure compliance and maintain ethical practices.

1. Data Protection and Privacy Laws

- GDPR (General Data Protection Regulation): A critical regulation in EU law concerning data protection and privacy for individuals within the European Union and the European Economic Area. It also addresses the transfer of personal data outside these regions, imposing stringent requirements on data handling and user consent.

- CCPA (California Consumer Privacy Act): This act enhances privacy rights and consumer protection for residents of California, USA. It grants consumers new rights with respect to the collection of their personal data by businesses operating in California.

- PIPEDA (Personal Information Protection and Electronic Documents Act): Canada's federal privacy law for the private sector, PIPEDA sets out the rules for how businesses must handle personal information in the course of commercial activity.

2. AI Ethics and Fairness Guidelines

- EU Ethics Guidelines for Trustworthy AI: These guidelines offer a framework for achieving trustworthy AI, emphasizing human autonomy, harm prevention, fairness, and transparency among other key principles.

- OECD Principles on AI: Developed and adopted by multiple countries, these principles aim to ensure that AI systems are designed and used in a way that is innovative, trustworthy, and respects human rights and democratic values.

3. E-commerce Specific Regulations

- E-commerce Directive (EU): A legal framework by the European Union that regulates online services, including issues like commercial communication and electronic contracts, to ensure a balanced and fair digital market.

- Consumer Protection Regulations: Different countries implement regulations to protect online consumers. These regulations often cover digital payment security, product quality assurance, and transparency in AI-based recommendations and advertising.

4. Intellectual Property Laws

- Copyright and Patent Laws: These laws are particularly relevant in protecting the intellectual property of AI algorithms and software, ensuring businesses maintain ownership and control over their technological innovations.

5. Export Controls and Trade Compliance

- Export Administration Regulations (EAR): In the U.S., these regulations control the export of dual-use items, which can include specific AI technologies with both civilian and military applications.

- International Traffic in Arms Regulations (ITAR): These U.S. regulations control the export and import of defense-related articles and services and can be applicable to certain specialized AI applications.

6. Anti-discrimination Laws

- ADA (Americans with Disabilities Act): This act is crucial for ensuring that AI-enhanced e-commerce platforms are accessible to individuals with disabilities, promoting inclusivity.

- Equal Employment Opportunity Laws: These laws are relevant when AI tools are employed in hiring and HR processes within e-commerce companies, ensuring non-discriminatory practices.

7. Sector-Specific Regulations

- Healthcare, Finance, and Insurance: E-commerce ventures operating within these sectors must adhere to specific regulations like HIPAA for healthcare in the U.S., or GDPR implications on financial data processing and privacy.

For e-commerce businesses utilizing AI and ML, navigating the regulatory landscape is complex but essential. Understanding and complying with these varied regulations and guidelines not only ensures legal compliance but also fortifies trust and ethical standing with consumers and partners. As technology and regulations continue to evolve, staying informed and agile in response to these changes will be key to successful and responsible operations in AI-enhanced e-commerce.

Appendix C:
Algorithmic Innovation: Optimizing E-commerce Supply Chains

E-commerce supply chains are increasingly reliant on algorithmic innovations to enhance efficiency and effectiveness. This appendix provides a comprehensive overview of key algorithms and their specific applications in optimizing various aspects of supply chain management in the e-commerce sector. Understanding these algorithms is crucial for businesses looking to leverage machine learning for improved operational performance.

Key Algorithms and Their Applications

Linear Regression

- Application: Primarily used for demand forecasting, linear regression models the relationship between sales and influencing factors such as price, seasonality, and market trends. This helps in predicting future sales volumes under different scenarios.

Logistic Regression

- Application: Utilized for predicting binary outcomes, such as determining the likelihood of a product being a best-seller, based on historical sales data and other relevant variables.

Decision Trees

- Application: Decision trees are employed for making structured decisions in inventory management and categorizing products according to sales patterns, customer demographics, or other relevant criteria.

Random Forests

- Application: An ensemble method that aggregates multiple decision trees for more accurate predictions. In supply chain management, random forests are used for enhanced demand forecasting and assessing risks associated with supply chain disruptions.

Neural Networks and Deep Learning

- Application: These complex algorithms are ideal for tasks like image recognition for product categorization and developing advanced demand forecasting models considering a multitude of variables.

Clustering Algorithms (like K-Means)

- Application: Crucial for customer segmentation, these algorithms help in tailoring marketing strategies, optimizing product placement, and personalizing customer experiences.

Natural Language Processing (NLP)

- Application: NLP is extensively used in customer service, powering chatbots for automated interactions and conducting sentiment analysis on customer feedback and reviews.

Time Series Analysis

- Application: Vital for forecasting future sales based on historical time-based data, aiding in inventory planning, and optimizing pricing strategies over different periods.

Reinforcement Learning

- Application: Effective in dynamic decision-making environments, such as real-time pricing models and automated logistics decision-making, adapting based on continuous feedback.

Support Vector Machines (SVM)

- Application: Used for classification tasks, SVMs are effective in fraud detection and predicting customer purchasing behaviors, contributing to enhanced security and targeted marketing.

Principal Component Analysis (PCA)

- Application: PCA is used for dimensionality reduction in large datasets, enhancing the efficiency and performance of other machine learning algorithms in processing complex supply chain data.

Genetic Algorithms

- Application: These are employed for solving complex optimization problems, such as determining the most efficient delivery routes or optimizing warehouse layouts for maximum efficiency.

Anomaly Detection Algorithms

- Application: Critical for identifying unusual patterns in supply chain data that may indicate fraud, operational inefficiencies, or potential disruptions.

This collection of algorithmic innovations underscores the wide-ranging applications of machine learning in enhancing e-commerce supply chain operations. By leveraging these algorithms, businesses can significantly improve efficiency, reduce costs, and heighten customer satisfaction. As technology continues to evolve, the potential for these algorithms to further transform supply chain management in the e-commerce sector is immense, paving the way for more innovative, responsive, and efficient supply chain solutions.

Appendix D:
The Essential AI Toolkit for Supply Chain Management

In the complex arena of e-commerce, effective supply chain management is crucial for success. Artificial Intelligence (AI) offers a suite of tools and technologies that are indispensable for optimizing these supply chains. This appendix provides a detailed overview of essential AI tools and technologies, elaborating on their functionalities and demonstrating how they can be strategically leveraged to streamline supply chain operations in the e-commerce sector.

1. Data Analytics Platforms

- Functionality: These platforms are essential for processing and analyzing large datasets, providing valuable insights about customer behaviors, market trends, and overall supply chain performance.

- Examples: Tableau for visual analytics, Microsoft Power BI for business intelligence, and Google Analytics for web analytics.

2. Machine Learning Frameworks

- Functionality: These frameworks are designed to develop, train, and deploy machine learning models that can efficiently predict market trends, demand patterns, and potential supply chain disruptions.

- Examples: TensorFlow for large-scale machine learning, PyTorch for complex computations, and Scikit-learn for data mining and analysis.

3. Inventory Management Software

- Functionality: AI in inventory management optimizes stock levels, automates replenishment processes, and reduces instances of overstocking or stockouts, ensuring efficient inventory control.

- Examples: Netsuite for integrated business management, Zoho Inventory for order and warehouse management, and Infor SCM for supply chain optimization.

4. Warehouse Management Systems (WMS)

- Functionality: These AI-powered systems enhance warehouse operations by automating picking processes, optimizing storage, and streamlining overall warehouse management.

- Examples: Manhattan WMS for warehouse fulfillment, Oracle Warehouse Management for cloud-based solutions, and SAP Extended Warehouse Management for comprehensive warehouse logistics.

5. Transportation Management Systems (TMS)

- Functionality: Leveraging AI for efficient transportation management, these systems assist in route optimization, carrier selection, and provide real-time tracking of shipments.

- Examples: JDA Transportation Management for supply chain planning, C.H. Robinson's Navisphere for global logistics, and MercuryGate TMS for transportation optimization.

6. Customer Relationship Management (CRM) Software

- Functionality: These tools, enhanced by AI, manage customer interactions, personalize communication, and improve customer service, fostering stronger customer relationships.

- Examples: Salesforce for customer engagement, HubSpot CRM for inbound marketing, and Zoho CRM for sales and marketing.

7. Predictive Analytics Tools

Functionality: These tools use AI to forecast future supply chain trends and behaviors, enabling businesses to make proactive, informed decisions.

Examples: SAS Predictive Analytics for advanced analytics, IBM SPSS for statistical analysis, and RapidMiner for data science.

8. Supply Chain Simulation Software

- Functionality: Simulation software allows businesses to model various supply chain scenarios, assessing potential outcomes and risks, thereby aiding strategic planning.

- Examples: AnyLogic for multi-method simulation, Simio for dynamic modeling, and FlexSim for 3D simulation.

9. IoT Platforms

- Functionality: Integrating IoT devices with AI enables real-time monitoring and data collection throughout the supply chain, enhancing visibility and responsiveness.

- Examples: Microsoft Azure IoT for IoT solutions, Cisco IoT Cloud Connect for connectivity management, and IBM Watson IoT for intelligent IoT.

10. Blockchain Technology

- Functionality: Blockchain technology offers a secure, transparent ledger system for supply chain transactions, enhancing traceability, reducing fraud, and increasing trust.

- Examples: Hyperledger for open-source blockchain frameworks, Ethereum for decentralized applications, and IBM Blockchain for business solutions.

The tools and technologies outlined in this appendix represent the cornerstone of AI in modern supply chain management, especially in the e-commerce context. By effectively leveraging these AI solutions, businesses can enhance operational efficiency, adapt to market changes, and ultimately deliver a superior customer experience. As these technologies continue to evolve, their role in revolutionizing supply chain management will become increasingly significant, shaping the future of e-commerce operations.

Appendix E:
AI in Action: Supply Chain Successes and Lessons Learned

The implementation of Artificial Intelligence (AI) in supply chain management has transformed operations in the e-commerce industry. This appendix presents real-world examples of successful AI applications, highlighting key successes, lessons learned, and providing insights for businesses aiming to integrate AI into their supply chain strategies.

1. Amazon: Pioneering Automated Warehousing and Dynamic Pricing

- Success: Amazon revolutionized warehousing with automated robots and implemented AI-driven dynamic pricing.

- Lessons Learned: The integration of AI with human labor needs to be seamless. Continuous refinement of algorithms is essential to adapt to market changes and optimize pricing strategies.

2. Walmart: Streamlining Inventory Management and Demand Forecasting

- Success: Walmart utilized AI for precise inventory management and accurate demand forecasting, enhancing supply chain efficiency.

- Lessons Learned: The effectiveness of AI depends on the quality of data. AI's role in reducing overstock and stockouts highlighted the importance of accurate inventory predictions.

3. Zara: Fast Fashion Meets Advanced Supply Chain Optimization

- Success: Zara applied AI in quick response management, enabling rapid turnover of new fashion lines and optimizing the supply chain.

- Lessons Learned: AI is advantageous in aligning production with current fashion trends and consumer demands, ensuring timely market responsiveness.

4. Maersk: Enhancing Global Shipping and Logistics with AI

- Success: Maersk implemented AI for route optimization and predictive maintenance, improving efficiency in global shipping logistics.

- Lessons Learned: AI enhances operational efficiency and can reduce environmental impacts through optimized shipping routes and preventative maintenance.

5. FedEx: Streamlined Package Sorting and Efficient Route Planning

- Success: FedEx integrated AI and robotics for effective package sorting and employed AI algorithms for smart route planning.

- Lessons Learned: The combination of robotics and AI can drastically increase processing speeds and accuracy, thereby boosting overall operational efficiency.

6. Alibaba: Empowering Smaller Retailers with Cloud-Based AI Solutions

- Success: Alibaba provided cloud-based AI solutions to small and medium-sized retailers, assisting them with demand forecasting and customer service.

- Lessons Learned: Cloud-based AI solutions can democratize technology access, enabling smaller businesses to adopt advanced capabilities and compete more effectively.

7. DHL: Proactive Logistics Forecasting and Risk Management

- Success: DHL utilized AI for logistics forecasting and risk management, proactively addressing potential disruptions.

- Lessons Learned: AI's predictive power is crucial in navigating risks and uncertainties, especially in complex, global supply chains.

8. Nike: AI-Driven Product Design and Market Analysis

- Success: Nike leveraged AI for innovative product design and market analysis, crafting targeted marketing strategies.

- Lessons Learned: AI can significantly contribute to product development and market positioning by comprehensively analyzing consumer behavior and trends.

These examples demonstrate that AI has become an indispensable tool in modern supply chain management, offering solutions that significantly enhance efficiency, responsiveness, and strategic decision-making. The key lessons learned from these pioneers in AI implementation reveal the importance of data quality, the need for continuous algorithmic refinement, and the benefits of adopting AI for predictive analysis and operational optimization. As AI technology continues to advance, its role in transforming supply chain management will undoubtedly expand, offering even more innovative and effective solutions for the e-commerce industry.

Appendix F:
Excellence in AI for Supply Chains: Model Evaluation and Impact

Incorporating Artificial Intelligence (AI) into supply chain management necessitates not only the development but also the rigorous evaluation of AI models. This appendix delves into the methods for evaluating AI models in supply chains and discusses the impact of effective AI implementation. It provides insights into ensuring that AI interventions are both efficient and beneficial to supply chain operations.

1. Key Performance Indicators (KPIs) for AI Model Evaluation

- Evaluation Metrics: Common metrics include accuracy, precision, recall, and F1 score for classification models. For regression models, metrics like Mean Absolute Error (MAE) and Root Mean Squared Error (RMSE) are used.

- Real-world Performance: Assessing how AI models perform in real operational environments, including their adaptability and robustness to changes in data patterns and market conditions.

2. Impact of AI on Supply Chain Efficiency

- Operational Efficiency: Examining the impact of AI on reducing lead times, optimizing inventory levels, and improving overall operational workflows.

- Cost Reduction: Evaluating AI's role in decreasing operational and logistics costs, including savings from reduced waste and improved resource allocation.

3. AI's Role in Enhancing Decision Making

- Data-Driven Insights: How AI contributes to making more informed, data-backed decisions in supply chain management.

- Predictive and Prescriptive Analytics: The effectiveness of AI models in not only predicting future trends but also prescribing actionable strategies for supply chain optimization.

4. Assessing AI's Contribution to Customer Satisfaction

- Improving Delivery and Fulfillment: Measuring AI's impact on enhancing delivery speed, accuracy, and the overall customer fulfillment process.

- Personalization: The role of AI in personalizing customer experiences, including tailored product recommendations and customized communication.

5. AI in Risk Management and Compliance

- Risk Prediction and Mitigation: The effectiveness of AI in identifying potential risks, from market fluctuations to supply chain disruptions, and proposing mitigation strategies.

- Compliance Monitoring: AI's role in ensuring supply chain practices comply with regulatory standards and ethical guidelines.

6. Sustainability and Environmental Impact

- Eco-friendly Logistics: Assessing how AI contributes to creating more sustainable logistics practices, such as route optimization for reduced emissions.

- Resource Optimization: The role of AI in minimizing resource usage and waste throughout the supply chain.

7. Challenges in AI Model Implementation

- Data Privacy and Security: Addressing concerns related to data privacy and security in AI implementations.

- Scalability and Integration: Challenges in scaling AI solutions and integrating them with existing supply chain systems and processes.

The evaluation and impact assessment of AI models in supply chains are crucial for ensuring their effectiveness and alignment with business goals. Proper evaluation methodologies and impact analyses help in realizing the full potential of AI, driving improvements in efficiency, decision-making, customer satisfaction, and sustainability. As AI continues to advance, its strategic implementation and evaluation in supply chain management will play a pivotal role in shaping the future of e-commerce operations.

Appendix G:
Sustainable Supply Chains: The Role of ML in Eco-Friendly Practices

In an era where environmental sustainability is paramount, the integration of Machine Learning (ML) into supply chain management has emerged as a transformative approach for e-commerce businesses. This appendix delves into how ML contributes to the development of sustainable supply chains, outlining its diverse applications and the environmental benefits it brings.

1. Enhanced Logistics and Transportation Efficiency

- Application: ML algorithms optimize logistics routes, minimizing fuel consumption and greenhouse gas emissions. These algorithms analyze vast amounts of data, including traffic patterns, delivery frequencies, and vehicle capacities, to create the most efficient delivery schedules and routes.

- Benefits: Reduced carbon footprint of logistics operations, lower fuel costs, and enhanced operational efficiency.

2. Advanced Inventory Management

- Application: ML assists in accurate inventory forecasting, reducing overproduction and excess stock. By analyzing past sales data, market trends, and consumer behavior, ML models can predict optimal inventory levels, thereby minimizing waste and the environmental impact of storage and disposal.

- Benefits: Decreased resource wastage, reduced storage costs, and lower environmental impact due to overproduction.

3. Sustainable Packaging Optimization

- Application: ML algorithms are employed to design environmentally friendly packaging solutions. These solutions take into account product dimensions, transportation requirements, and material recyclability to minimize waste and maximize the use of sustainable materials.

- Benefits: Reduction in packaging waste, increased use of sustainable packaging materials, and minimized environmental impact.

4. Waste Management and Recycling Enhancement

- Application: ML is used to analyze and improve waste management and recycling processes. This includes optimizing collection routes, automating waste sorting, and identifying the most effective recycling strategies.

- Benefits: Improved efficiency of recycling processes, reduced landfill waste, and enhanced conservation of resources.

5. Energy Consumption Reduction in Warehousing

- Application: ML tools analyze energy usage patterns in warehouses and distribution centers to identify opportunities for energy savings, such as automating lighting and climate control systems based on real-time occupancy and weather data.

- Benefits: Decreased energy consumption, reduced greenhouse gas emissions, and cost savings on energy expenses.

6. Sustainable Supplier Evaluation

- Application: ML assists in evaluating and selecting suppliers based on their sustainability practices. It analyzes data regarding suppliers' environmental impact, ethical standards, and resource utilization.

- Benefits: Encourages ethical sourcing, supports eco-friendly suppliers, and ensures the sustainability of the supply chain.

7. Predicting Demand for Eco-Friendly Products

- Application: ML algorithms predict consumer demand for sustainable products, helping businesses align their product offerings with market trends and consumer preferences for environmentally friendly options.

- Benefits: Drives the supply of sustainable products, meets consumer demand for eco-friendly options, and fosters sustainable consumption.

Machine Learning is a key enabler in fostering sustainable practices within e-commerce supply chains. From optimizing logistics to enhancing energy efficiency and promoting sustainable sourcing, ML's applications are diverse and impactful. As the global focus on environmental sustainability intensifies, the role of ML in driving eco-friendly supply chain practices becomes increasingly crucial. This technology not only supports businesses in reducing their environmental footprint but also in aligning with the growing consumer demand for sustainability, marking a significant stride towards a more responsible and sustainable e-commerce ecosystem.

Appendix H:
Predictive Analytics: Forecasting Demand and Inventory Management

Predictive analytics, a cornerstone of modern supply chain management, particularly in e-commerce, has become increasingly crucial in forecasting demand and optimizing inventory management. This appendix delves into the role of predictive analytics in these key areas, highlighting its significance, methodologies, and impacts on supply chain efficiency.

1. The Essence of Predictive Analytics in Demand Forecasting

- Application: Predictive analytics involves using historical data, machine learning algorithms, and statistical models to forecast future customer demand. By analyzing past sales trends, market conditions, and consumer behavior patterns, businesses can anticipate future product demands.

- Benefits: Enhanced ability to meet customer demand, optimized production planning, and reduced risk of stockouts or excess inventory.

2. Techniques and Models Used in Demand Forecasting

- Time Series Analysis: Utilizes historical data over time to predict future demand. Common models include ARIMA (AutoRegressive Integrated Moving Average) and exponential smoothing.

- Regression Analysis: Helps in understanding how various factors like pricing, promotions, and economic indicators influence demand.

- Machine Learning Models: Algorithms such as decision trees, neural networks, and ensemble methods are employed to capture complex, non-linear relationships in data.

3. Predictive Analytics in Inventory Management

- Application: Predictive analytics optimizes inventory levels by predicting the optimal amount of stock required to meet forecasted demand. It helps in automating replenishment decisions and identifying potential inventory-related issues before they occur.

- Benefits: Reduced carrying costs, minimized risk of overstocking or stockouts, and improved cash flow management.

4. Data Sources and Quality in Predictive Analytics

Data Sources: Key data sources include historical sales data, customer transaction records, market trend data, and supplier performance metrics.

Data Quality: The accuracy of predictive analytics is heavily dependent on the quality, completeness, and relevance of the data used. Clean, well-structured, and up-to-date data is essential for reliable forecasting.

5. Challenges and Considerations in Implementing Predictive Analytics

- Integrating Diverse Data Sources: Effectively integrating and harmonizing data from various sources can be challenging but is crucial for accurate forecasting.

- Balancing Accuracy and Timeliness: Achieving a balance between the accuracy of predictions and the need for timely decision-making is vital.

- Adapting to Market Changes: Predictive models must be regularly updated and refined to adapt to changing market conditions and consumer behaviors.

Predictive analytics has become an indispensable tool in e-commerce for forecasting demand and managing inventory efficiently. Its ability to analyze vast datasets and predict future trends offers significant advantages, including enhanced responsiveness to market demand, optimized inventory levels, and improved overall supply chain efficiency. As technology and data analytics continue to advance, the role of predictive analytics in shaping efficient and responsive supply chains is set to grow even more integral, offering businesses a competitive edge in the ever-evolving landscape of e-commerce.

Appendix I:
Future Trends: AI and the Evolving Landscape of E-commerce Logistics

The landscape of e-commerce logistics is rapidly evolving, largely driven by advancements in Artificial Intelligence (AI). This appendix explores the future trends in AI that are expected to significantly influence e-commerce logistics, offering insights into how these innovations could reshape the industry.

1. Enhanced Automation in Warehousing and Delivery

- Future Trends: The integration of AI with robotics in warehousing will lead to more sophisticated automated storage and retrieval systems. In delivery, the use of drones and autonomous vehicles for last-mile delivery is anticipated to grow.

- Implications: These advancements will lead to faster order processing, reduced operational costs, and increased efficiency in delivery services.

2. Advanced Real-Time Decision Making

- Future Trends: AI will enable more complex real-time decision-making capabilities in logistics management, including dynamic routing and instant rerouting in response to unexpected events.

- Implications: Enhanced responsiveness and agility in supply chain operations, leading to improved customer satisfaction and operational resilience.

3. Predictive and Prescriptive Analytics

- Future Trends: Beyond forecasting, AI will advance towards prescriptive analytics, offering actionable recommendations and automated decision-making based on predictive data insights.

- Implications: More proactive management of supply chain risks, optimization of inventory levels, and improved planning strategies.

4. Personalized Customer Experiences

- Future Trends: AI will drive more personalized logistics experiences, such as customized delivery options, predictive ordering, and personalized product recommendations based on individual customer data.

- Implications: Increased customer engagement and loyalty, and a more tailored e-commerce experience for consumers.

5. Sustainable and Green Logistics

- Future Trends: AI will play a critical role in developing sustainable logistics solutions, optimizing routes for minimal environmental impact, and facilitating the use of eco-friendly packaging materials and processes.

- Implications: Reduction in carbon footprint of logistics operations, alignment with global sustainability goals, and enhanced corporate social responsibility.

6. Enhanced Supply Chain Collaboration and Transparency

- Future Trends: AI technologies will foster greater collaboration and transparency across the supply chain network, utilizing blockchain and other technologies to share data securely and efficiently.

- Implications: Improved trust among supply chain partners, enhanced data integrity, and more efficient coordination across the supply chain.

7. Integration with Emerging Technologies

- Future Trends: AI will increasingly integrate with other emerging technologies such as the Internet of Things (IoT), 5G connectivity, and blockchain to create more interconnected and intelligent supply chain systems.

- Implications: Seamless data flow and enhanced interconnectivity leading to smarter, more responsive supply chains.

The future of e-commerce logistics, underpinned by AI, holds tremendous promise for transforming the industry. From enhanced automation and real-time decision-making to sustainable practices and personalized customer experiences, these advancements are poised to redefine the efficiency, agility, and responsiveness of e-commerce logistics. As AI continues to advance, staying abreast of these trends will be crucial for businesses looking to remain competitive and innovative in the dynamic landscape of e-commerce.